Leo the Late Bloomer

BY ROBERT KRAUS • PICTURES BY JOSE ARUEGO

Prentice-Hall Books for Young Readers
A Division of Simon & Schuster, Inc.
New York

For Ken Dewey

and

For Pamela, Bruce and Billy

Text copyright © 1971 by Robert Kraus
Illustrations copyright © 1971 by Jose Aruego
All rights reserved including the right of reproduction
in whole or in part in any form.
Published by Prentice-Hall Books for Young Readers
A Division of Simon & Schuster, Inc.
Simon & Schuster Building
Rockefeller Center
1230 Avenue of the Americas
New York, NY 10020

10 9 8 7 6 5 4 3 2   pbk

Originally published by Windmill Books, Inc.
Prentice-Hall Books for Young Readers is a
trademark of Simon & Schuster, Inc.
Manufactured in the United States of America

Library of Congress Cataloging in Publication Data
Kraus, Robert, 1925-
    Leo the late bloomer.
    Summary: Leo, a young tiger, finally blooms under the anxious eyes of his parents.
    [1. Tigers—Fiction]   I. Aruego, Jose.
II. Title.
[PZ7.K868Le   1980]   [E]   80-12511
ISBN 0-13-530288-9 pbk

Leo couldn't do anything right.

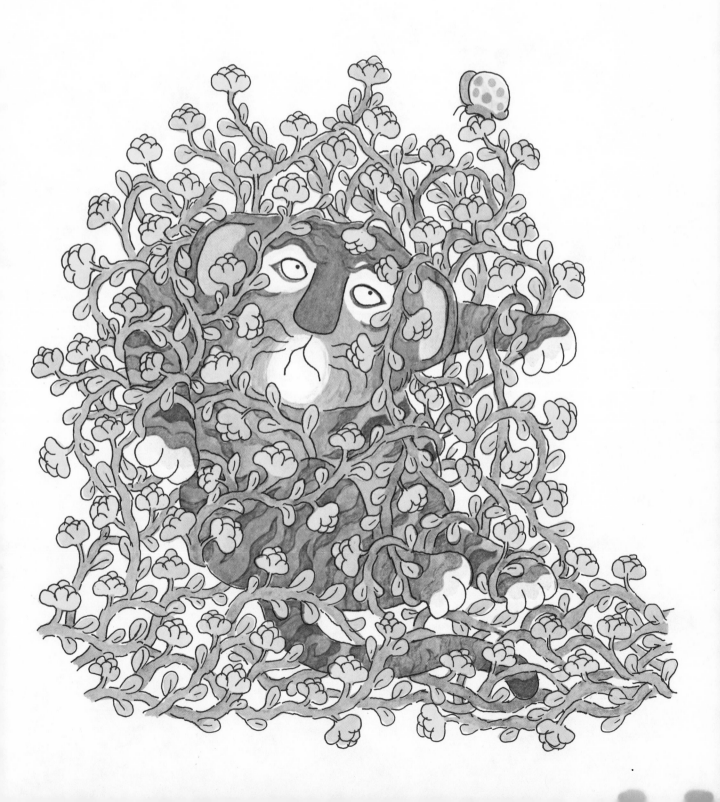

He couldn't read.

He couldn't write.

owl
Elephant
Snake
Plover
Crocodile

He couldn't draw.

He was a sloppy eater.

And, he never said a word.

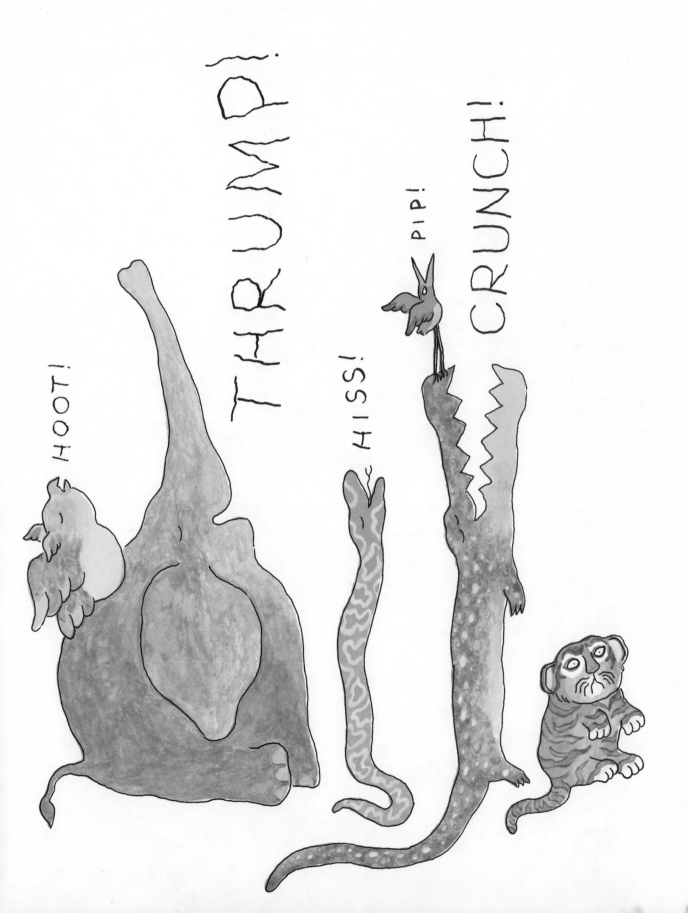

"What's the matter with Leo?"
asked Leo's father.
"Nothing," said Leo's mother.
"Leo is just a late bloomer."
"Better late than never," thought Leo's father.

Every day Leo's father watched him
for signs of blooming.

And every night Leo's father watched him
for signs of blooming.

"Are you sure Leo's a bloomer?"
asked Leo's father.
"Patience," said Leo's mother,
"A watched bloomer doesn't bloom."

So Leo's father watched television
instead of Leo.

The snows came.
Leo's father wasn't watching.
But Leo still wasn't blooming.

The trees budded.
Leo's father wasn't watching.
But Leo still wasn't blooming.

Then one day,
in his own good time,
Leo bloomed!

He could read !

He could write!

He could draw!

He ate neatly!

He also spoke.
And it wasn't just a word.
It was a whole sentence.
And that sentence was...

"I made it!"

the ETC program

Cross-Cultural Communication

A Competency-Based Grammar

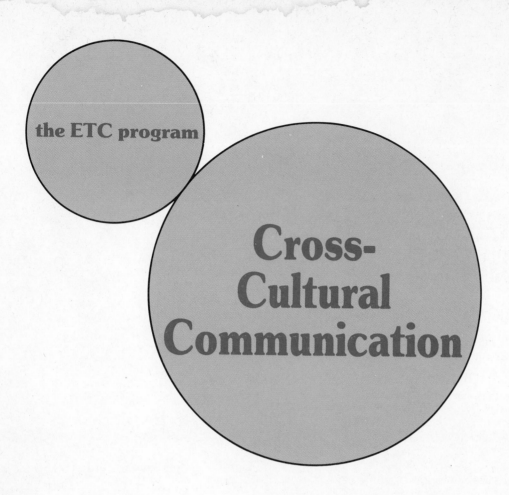

the ETC program

Cross-Cultural Communication

A Competency-Based Grammar

Pamela Hartmann

Evans Community Adult School
Los Angeles Unified School District

RANDOM HOUSE New York

First Edition

9 8 7 6 5 4 3 2

Copyright © 1989 by Random House, Inc.

Library of Congress Cataloging-in-Publication Data

Hartmann, Pamela.
    The *ETC* program. Cross-cultural communication;
    a competency-based grammar.
    Level 4.
    1. English language—Textbooks for foreign speakers.
2. English language—Grammar—1950— . 3. Intercultural communication.
PE1128.H38   1988   428.2′4   88-18215
ISBN 0-394-35350-1 (Student Edition)
ISBN 0-394-38065-7 (Teacher's Edition)

Manufactured in the United States of America

Series design and production: Etcetera Graphics
                                   Canoga Park, California

Cover design: Juan Vargas, Vargas/Williams Design

Illustrations: Etcetera Graphics

Artist: Terry Wilson

Photo Research: Marian Hartsough

Photos: Sally Gati

Typesetting: Etcetera Graphics

Contents

Preface

To learn another language is to enter a new world.
—*Cherry Vasconcellos*

About the *ETC* Program

ETC is a six-level ESL (English as a second language) program for adults who are learning English to improve their lives and work skills. The material of this level is divided into three books, carefully coordinated, chapter by chapter, in theme, competency goals, grammar, and vocabulary. Each text can be used independently or in conjunction with one or both of the other two. For a visual representation of the scope and sequence of the program, see the back cover of any volume.

About This Book

ETC Cross-Cultural Communication: A Competency-Based Grammar is an intermediate grammar text for adult students of English as a second language. It aims at helping students attain competency not only in the grammar of the language but also in the practical aspects of daily life in North America. (For a description of the abilities of typical learners who would benefit most from this text, see the introduction to the accompanying instructor's manual—"About This Level.")

Organization

Like most other books in the *ETC* program, this volume consists of an introduction and ten chapters. The chapters are divided into four parts, each of which has a specific grammatical focus. A pretest opens each chapter; these exercises are to give students a preview of the grammar presented in the chapter and to help them identify what they already know and what they need to learn. A similiar, slightly more challenging test is included in the instructor's edition. These can be duplicated and given to students as a means of measuring what they have learned. A large asterisk, or star, marks optional exercises called "Beyond the book."

Available Ancillaries

The instructor's manual for this text includes:

- a general introduction to the *ETC* program, this level, and this book

- suggestions for teaching techniques to use in presenting the various kinds of activities

- an answer key for text exercises

Acknowledgments

Much appreciation and thanks go to:

—those who made this book possible:

Elaine Kirn, originator and coordinator of the series
Eirik Borve, Mary McVey Gill, and the staff at Random House, and Sally
Kostal, Chuck Alessio, Tony Thorne-Booth, and the staff at Etcetera Graphics;

—those who gave time, expertise, and help with research:

Fusako Ohtani Haverty, Planaria Price, JoAnne Shayne, Annette Zarian, and
Dr. Ruben Zarian;

—the following reviewers, whose comments, both favorable and critical, were of
great value in the development of *ETC Cross-Cultural Communication*:

Betsy Baily, Joseph Berkowitz, Laurie Blass, Lori B. Brooks, Robert Gear,
Renee Klosz, Nick Kremer, Emily Lites, Saul Sanchez, Peggy Seufert-Bosco,
Libby Shanefield, Kent Sutherland, and Ann Wederspahn;

and

—friends and relations who put up with me through it all.

P.H.

Parts of Speech

Introduction

GRAMMAR:
Nouns, adjectives, and
  prepositions
Transitive and intransitive
  verbs

COMPETENCIES:
Naming things
Describing things and people
Describing where things are

Adjectives			Nouns	
angry	international	sick	board	desk
bored	messy	sleepy	child	man
busy	neat	sunny	city	person/people
confused	nervous	tall	classroom	receptionist
crowded	nice	unhappy	clinic	street
full	old	young	day	woman
happy	short			

 A. Tell what you see in the pictures at the beginning of this section. Use adjectives and nouns from the list above and words of your own. (You can work in small groups.)

EXAMPLES: (Picture 2) a young receptionist
                               sick people
                               an unhappy child

Subject	Transitive Verb (needs object)	Object
I	like	this neighborhood.
You	don't need	an appointment.
She	has	a cold.
Her friend	enjoys	school.
He sometimes	hurts[1]	his arm when he plays tennis.
We usually	understand[1]	the teacher.
Jack and I	take	classes at this school.
They	want	a registration card.
Mike and Alice	introduce	their friends.

Subject	Intransitive Verb (does not need object)	
I	don't understand.[1]	
You	work	hard.
She	comes	from Canada.
My stomach	hurts.[1]	
We	live[1]	over there.
They	relax[1]	after class.
Children	cry	when they're afraid.

[1] Some verbs can be either transitive or intransitive.

B. Make sentences about the pictures at the beginning of this section. Use verbs from the box above and use your imagination.

EXAMPLES: (Picture 2) A man has a headache.
                               She works in a clinic.
                               Maybe that woman comes from my country.

Prepositions (of place)

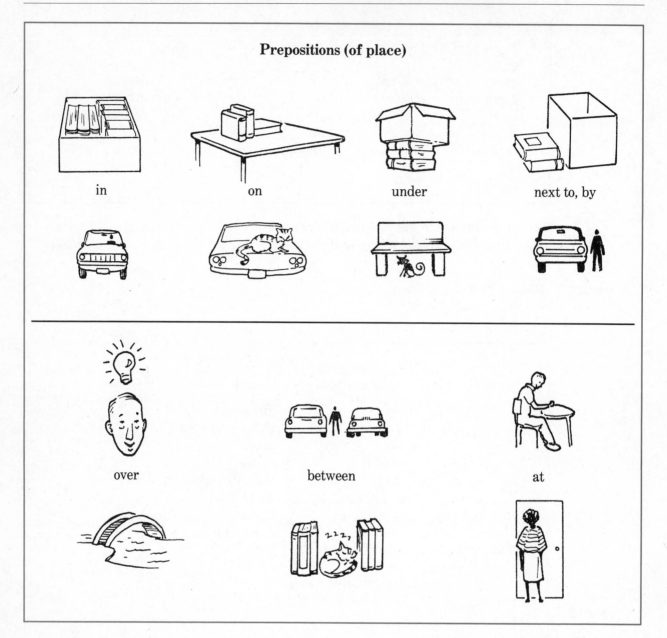

    in   on   under   next to, by

over   between   at

_____ **C.**   **Make sentences about the people and things in the pictures at the beginning of this section. Use prepositions from the box above to tell where they are.**

EXAMPLES: (Picture 2)   People are on a sofa.
                          A receptionist is at her desk.
                          Some magazines are on a table.

_____ ***D.**   **Beyond the book: Look around your classroom and tell what you see. Use adjectives to describe things and people, and prepositions to tell where they are.**

EXAMPLES: A tall student is next to me.
                 A yellow pencil is on that desk.
                 New students are at the door.

Beginnings

GRAMMAR:
The present continuous and
  simple present tenses:
    Statements
    Questions
Simple modals of permission
  and request
it/there (with weather)
Frequency words

COMPETENCIES:
Understanding procedures
  for registering for classes
Making small talk
Reading and asking questions
  about class schedules
Asking for permission
Making requests
Stating weather conditions
Describing problems with
  homesickness

Students and teachers get acquainted.

How much do you already know? **Read the following paragraphs and choose the correct words. Circle your answers.**

At the beginning of each semester, the International School of English always [has / is having]
enterarse, conocer   1.
a get-acquainted party. At these parties, new students [get / are getting] the chance to meet each
                                                                                            2.
other and to meet returning students and teachers.

Today, they [hold / are holding] the party outside on the campus because [it / there] is a
                    3.   4.
beautiful day.

There are many students [wear / wearing] traditional clothing from their countries at this
                                              5.
party. Right now, people from various countries [greet / are greeting] each other in different ways.
                                                                    saludar   6.
[It / There] is a woman over there [shakes / shaking] hands with a man. Two men [bow / are
7. *inclinarse saludar*   8. *abrazar*   9.
bowing] to each other. One person [hugs / is hugging] another, and another man is kissing
                                                            10.
someone on the cheek. Everyone [is / are] making "small talk" (polite conversation).
                                              11.

Sometimes there are problems at these get-acquainted parties because polite small talk
difiere
[differs / is differing] from culture to culture. At parties in most cultures, people's first topic of
12.
small talk is the weather, or the party, or a person's type of work. But in some cultures, one person
desconocido
[asks often / often asks] a stranger or new acquaintance, "Are you married?" or "How much money
13.
[you make / do you make]?" or "What religion [your family believes in / does your family believe
14.   15.
in]?" or "[You have / Do you have] a boyfriend?" People from some countries, such as the United
                    16.
States, [don't feel usually / don't usually feel] comfortable with such questions from strangers. But
            17.
at the International School of English, everybody tries to learn about each other's customs, so there
raro-rez
are seldom any serious problems.

Everybody [comes / is coming] to school on Tuesday for the first day of class, and registration
                            18.
[begins / beginning] at 9:00 on Monday. Now students [enjoy / are enjoying] one of their last days
19.   20.
of vacation.

calificación
score: _____
20

PART ONE

The Present Continuous and Simple Present Tenses: Statements

● Understanding Procedures for Registering for Classes

The Present Continuous Tense: Statements

Subject	*be* (*not*)	Verb-*ing*
I	am	registering for class.
You	are	standing next to me.
That man	is not	enjoying the long wait.
Everyone	is[1]	checking the schedule of classes.
They	are not	making small talk.
Two girls	are	smiling and waving.[2]

[1] Words such as *everyone* and *group* mean "several" (or many), but such words are singular.

[2] When there are two verbs of the same tense in a sentence, don't repeat the verb *be* if you don't repeat the subject.

Contractions

Use contractions when possible, especially in conversation. They sound more natural than the full forms do.

I'm	I'm not
you're	you're not (you aren't)
he's	he's not (he isn't)
she's	she's not (she isn't)
it's	it's not (it isn't)
we're	we're not (we aren't)
they're	they're not (they aren't)

Uses   Expressions

Use the present continuous tense for:

1. an action that is happening right now ⟶ now / right now / at this moment

2. a temporary action or an action in the period around the present moment ⟶ today / this week / these days / temporarily

3. plans for the future ⟶ tomorrow / next week / next Friday

A. Use the underlined words to make affirmative (+) and negative (–) sentences in the present continuous tense.

EXAMPLE: 1. New students are getting acquainted with each other.

1. New students / <u>get</u> acquainted with each other. (+)

2. Several people / <u>introduce</u> themselves to others. (+)

3. A returning student / <u>introduce</u> a new student to a teacher. (+)

4. People / <u>worry</u> about exams and homework yet. (–)

5. Everyone / <u>hope</u> to learn a lot about the other students' cultures (+ –)

   this semester, and no one / <u>feel</u> homesick yet.

6. Several new students / <u>talk</u> about the placement exam that they / <u>take</u> (+ +)

   next Monday morning.

The Simple Present Tense: Statements

Subject	*do (not)*[1]	Verb
I		study here.
You		speak English.
The student		likes it here.
She	does not	know anyone yet.
They		come every day.
The classes	do not	meet on Saturdays.

Uses   **Expressions**

Use the simple present tense for:

1. a repeated activity   ———► every day (every week, month, etc.)/
                                                        usually/often/sometimes/seldom/
                                                        all the time   *noro-vez*

2. a situation that is always true ——► always/never/not ever *algua vez*

3. scheduled events in the future[2] ——► tomorrow/next week (next Thursday,
                                                          month, etc.)

[1]Contractions (*don't, doesn't*) are more common   [2]Use the simple present tense in this way only
than the full form.   with certain verbs, such as *start, begin, end,*
                                                                               open, close, arrive, leave.

B. **Use the following words to make affirmative (+) and negative (–) sentences in the simple present tense.**

EXAMPLE: **1.** The director of the school usually makes a short welcoming speech at these parties.

1. The director of the school usually / <u>make</u> a short welcoming speech at these   (+)
parties.

2. Everyone always / <u>listen</u>, but sometimes they / <u>understand</u> because he /   (+–+)

<u>speak</u> fast.

3. Every year, new students soon / <u>learn</u> to communicate with a smile and   (+–)

"body language," so they / <u>need</u> to worry.

_____ **C.** **Make sentences about the picture. Use the present continuous tense to tell what is happening right now. Use as many of the verbs under the picture as possible.**

EXAMPLE: Students are enrolling in classes right now.

enroll	stand	take	read	shrug	ask	wait
register	go	yawn	talk	check	give	walk

1. _every one is stand up._
2. _students are toke Placement clamen._
3. _Mony shutents are reding the schedule of classes_
4. _every day the students wait in the classroom._
5. _every year. they're register their names._
6. _sometime they go to the cafeteria._
7. _In the murning they wait in the line_
8. _the student all the time are yawning_

D. **Look at the picture again. Make sentences in the simple present tense to tell what happens every semester at this school.**

EXAMPLE: Every semester, students stand in line to enroll in classes.

1. _____

2. _____

3. _____

4. _____

5. _____

6. _____

7. _____

8. _____

E. **Make sentences with the cue words. Use the present continuous and simple present tenses of the underlined words. Follow the example.**

EXAMPLE: 1. Freddy is looking at the schedule of classes right now.
Every semester he checks for changes in the schedule.
He doesn't usually have a problem with his schedule.

1. **Freddy**
   <u>look</u> at the schedule of classes right now
   every semester <u>check</u> for schedule changes
   <u>not</u> usually <u>have</u> a problem with his schedule

2. **Wendy Lim**
   <u>register</u> for classes at this moment
   usually <u>take</u> two English classes
   sometimes <u>need</u> to put her name on a waiting list

3. **Ana Maria**
   <u>talk</u> with a counselor right now
   always <u>like</u> to get advice before she registers
   usually <u>have</u> questions in mind when she <u>see</u> him

4. Dorothy Anderson
<u>teach</u> Level 4 this semester
<u>not</u> usually <u>teach</u> this class
<u>teach</u> Level 3 most of the time

Course	Time	Days	Room	Instructor
ESL4	9:00	M-F	120	D. Anderson

5. several students
<u>try</u> to register for the computer class now
<u>not</u> always <u>get</u> in at the beginning of the semester
often <u>have</u> to check the waiting list every few days

6. Hal Roberts
<u>work</u> as a counselor this year
<u>give</u> a placement exam to new students every month
always <u>explain</u> that this exam <u>help</u> to put students in
    the right level

7. a few students
<u>buy</u> books at the student bookstore at this moment
<u>not</u> usually <u>do</u> this until after the first day of class
seldom <u>know</u> the books they need until their teachers
    <u>tell</u> them the titles

*F. **Beyond the book: Discuss or write about the beginning of the semester or quarter at your school. How do students register for classes? What problems do they sometimes have? What classes does your school offer? What's happening at your school today? What's happening this week?**

PART TWO   The Present Continuous and Simple Present Tenses: Questions

● Making Small Talk ● Reading and Asking Questions about Class Schedules

---

The Present Continuous Tense: Questions

If the answer to a question is the subject, *who* or *what* becomes the subject in the question. The present continuous tense follows this word. (Note: *Be* is usually singular, even if the answer is plural.)

Question Word (Subject)	be (not)	Verb-*ing* ?
Who	is	shaking hands?
(Answer: Two students	are	shaking hands.)
What	is	happening?
(Answer: Nothing much	is	happening.)

If the answer to a question is the verb, object, place, time, or anything except the subject, use the subject in the question, between the verb *be* and verb-*ing*.

Question Word	be (not)	Subject	Verb-*ing* ?
What	are	you	doing?
(Answer:		I'm	registering.)
Who	is	she	meeting?
(Answer:		She's	meeting a counselor.)
	Are	they	taking ESL 5?
(Answer: (No.		They're	taking ESL 4.)

 A. The students in the following conversation are friends who are in different classes this semester. It's the third day of class. They're making small talk during their break. Make a question for each answer. Use the present continuous tense; don't use any underlined words. (The underlined words are the answers.)

EXAMPLE: Mrs. Lopez: How are you feeling?
Mrs. Wang: I'm feeling better, thanks.

1. Mrs. Lopez: _____

Mrs. Wang: I'm taking ESL 3.

2. Mrs. Lopez: _____

Mrs. Wang: It's going pretty well. How about you?

3. Mrs. Lopez: Everything's okay. I like my typing class. _____

_____

Mrs. Wang: Alan Murphy is teaching our Level 3 class.

4. Mrs. Lopez: Oh, good. _____

   Mrs. Wang: <u>Yes</u>, he's giving us <u>a lot of</u> homework this semester! I'm looking forward to the weekend—and a chance to rest!

   Mrs. Lopez: Oh, me too! We're having a family picnic on Sunday.

5. Mrs. Wang: _____

   Mrs. Lopez: We're going <u>to Summerville Park</u>.

6. Mrs. Wang: _____

   Mrs. Lopez: <u>My husband and kids</u> are doing all the cooking.

   Mrs. Wang: Ah! That's why you're looking forward to it!

7. Mrs. Lopez: Yes! _____

   Mrs. Wang: <u>No</u>, we're <u>not</u> going anywhere this weekend.

8. Mrs. Lopez: Sometimes it's wonderful to have a quiet weekend at home. _____

   _____

9. Mrs. Wang: <u>Yes</u>, I'm spending <u>a lot of</u> time in the garden these days. How about

   you? _____

   Mrs. Lopez: Our garden is doing <u>really well</u>. Our fruit trees have a lot of fruit this year.

The Simple Present Tense: Questions

If the answer to a question is the subject, there is only one verb in the question—the main verb, in the simple present tense.

Question Word (Subject)	Verb ?
Who	teaches that class?
(Answer: Mrs. Anderson	teaches it.)

If the answer to a question is the verb, object, place, time, or anything except the subject, use two verbs in the question: *do* or *does* and the simple form of the main verb. The subject comes between these verbs.

Question Word	*do/does*	Subject	Verb ?
What	does	he	teach?
(Answer:		He	teaches ESL.)
How often	do	you	have homework?
(Answer:		We	have it every day.)

B. The students in the following conversation are both new to the school and don't really know each other yet. They're in Level 4 together and are making small talk as they wait for the teacher to arrive. Make a question for each answer. Use the simple present tense; don't use any underlined words.

1. Cheung: _How do you like this class ?_____

   Roya: I like this class a lot. How about you?

   Cheung: Me too. But sometimes the vocabulary is hard. It's really different from my language.

2. Roya: _____

3. Cheung: I speak Chinese. And you? _____

   Roya: I come from Iran. School is hard for me, too, especially when I have to work full-time.

4. Cheung: _____

     Roya: I'm a waitress.

5. Cheung: _____

6.   Roya: No, I don't like it very much, but I hope to change jobs soon. And how about you? _____

     Cheung: Yes, I work part-time for my uncle, so I have enough time to take the computer programming class here, too.

7.   Roya: Oh? _____

     Cheung: A Canadian lady teaches it. I don't remember her name.

C. Look again at the picture on page 11. Make questions about it. Use the present continuous tense to ask about what is happening right now.

EXAMPLE: Why are those people standing in line?

1. _____

2. _____

3. _____

4. _____

5. _____

6. _____

D. Use the same picture to make questions about what happens at the beginning of every semester. Use the simple present tense.

EXAMPLE: Where do new students take the placement exam?

1. _____

2. _____

3. _____

4. _____

5. _____

6. _____

E. **Look at the schedule of classes below. Make questions about it. Use the present continuous and simple present tenses.**

EXAMPLES: What is Professor Murphy teaching this semester?

Do you usually need an appointment to see a counselor?

International School of English

SCHEDULE OF CLASSES

Course	Time	Days	Room	Instructor
ESL 1a	9:00 a.m.	M-F	217	R. Dawes
ESL 1b	6:30 p.m.	M-Th	119	P. Lim
ESL 2a	9:00 a.m.	M-F	214	C. Brown
ESL 2b	6:30 p.m.	T Th	106	M. Gable
ESL 3	7:00 p.m.	M-Th	309	A. Murphy
ESL 4	9:00 a.m.	M-F	120	D. Anderson
ESL 5	10:00 a.m.	M-F	217	R. Dawes
Typing	7:00 p.m.	M W F	201	A. Cohan
Computers	7:00 p.m.	T Th	202	D. Carr
Office Skills	7:00 p.m.	M-Th	203	M. Torres
Lang. Lab	10:00 a.m.	M-F	109	P. Lim
Lang. Lab	7:00 p.m.	M-F	109	N. Stein
Bank Teller Training	10:00 a.m.	T Th	203	T. Sato

Class Fees: $15 per class for city residents, $75 for nonresidents

Parking Fees: $10

Students *must* attend first class meeting, or they will be dropped from the course.

Bring the following to registration: a #2 Pencil, I.D. card.

Students *must* be at least 18 years of age to enroll.

Counselors see students by appointment only.

*F. **Beyond the book: Ask and answer questions about the beginning of school in other countries, other cities, or other schools. Use the present continuous and simple present tenses. (You may work in small groups.)**

EXAMPLES: a: Do you pay fees for classes in your country?

b: Well, high school is free, but college students pay a fee. We don't have adult school in my country.

PART THREE / Simple Modals of Permission and Request

● Asking for Permission ● Making Requests

Simple Modals

Permission	Request
To ask for permission, you usually use the subject I. Other subjects are possible, except for you; never use the subject you to ask for permission.	To request something, the subject is you. This is a very polite form of a command.

Modal	Subject	Verb ?
May	I please[1]	ask something?
Can	we	leave early?
Could	my brother	come[2] to class?

Modal	Subject	Verb ?
Could	you please[1]	lend me a pen?
Would	you	help us please?
Can	you please[1]	speak louder?
Will	you	open the door?

[1] The word *please* comes either after the subject or at the end of the sentence.

[2] The main verb after any modal is always in the simple form, but the "tense" of sentences of permission or request is present or future.

  A. **Use a modal and subject to complete each sentence below. (There might be several correct answers.)**

EXAMPLE: **1.** May I use my cassette recorder during class?

1. _____Can you_____ use my cassette recorder during class?

2. _____may you_____ hand me the sign-in sheet?

3. _____Would you_____ tell us a little about yourself?

4. _____may you_____ borrow your pencil for a second?

5. _____can you_____ please share your book just for today?

6. _____could you_____ please explain that again?

7. _____ come a few minutes late tomorrow?

8. _____ have an extra practice sheet, please?

9. _____ speak a little slower, please?

10. _____ help you carry that?

11. _____ help me with this?

12. _____ please open the window for us?

B. Freddy Xenos, a student at the International School of English, knows that it's important to be polite when he asks for something. What can he say in the following situations? Make questions with the correct modals and subjects.

EXAMPLES: **Situation 1:** May I please borrow some money?

Could you lend me some money?

Situation 1: Freddy is on the phone with his older brother, who lives in another city. Freddy isn't planning his budget very well, and he's spending too much money these days. He needs some extra money for rent this month. What can he ask his brother?

Permission: _____

Request: _____

Situation 2: Freddy is in class. He doesn't have a dictionary, and he needs one for just a minute. What can he ask the person next to him?

Permission: _____

Request: _____

Situation 3: Freddy is in class. He was absent yesterday, so he needs the papers that the teacher handed out then. What can he ask the teacher?

Permission: _____

Request: _____

Situation 4: Because Freddy was absent yesterday, he needs to copy the class notes that he missed. What can he ask Wendy Lim?

Permission: _____

Request: _____

Situation 5: Freddy is in the library and he wants to check out some books, but he doesn't have a library card. How can he ask the librarian for an application form for a library card?

Permission: _____

Request: _____

Situation 6: Freddy and some classmates are in a coffee shop. They're having a snack after class. When they want the check so that they can leave, what can they ask the waitress?

Permission: _____

Request: _____

_____ **C.** **Read each situation below and decide which kind of question to ask: permission or request. Then make one question for each situation. (The underlined words will help you decide who is the subject.)**

EXAMPLE: **Situation 1:** (request) Could you please tell me the time?

Situation 1: You're at a bus stop. You're waiting for the bus to school. You think the bus is late, but you're not sure because you don't have your watch on. You want <u>the person next to you</u> at the bus stop to tell you the time. What can you ask?

_____

Situation 2: You're new at this school, and you can't find the bookstore. You want <u>another student</u> to give you directions. What can you ask?

_____

Situation 3: You're walking into the bookstore. You see a teacher who is having difficulty with a heavy briefcase and a lot of books. <u>You</u> want to help. What do you ask?

_____

Situation 4: You're in the counseling office. <u>You</u> want an appointment with a counselor. What do you ask?

_____

Situation 5: You're in a class. You don't understand a grammar rule, and you want <u>the teacher</u> to explain it. What do you ask?

_____

Situation 6: You're in class. The room is almost full; there is only one empty seat, but there's a sweater on it. <u>You</u> want that seat. What can you ask the person in the next seat?

_____

Situation 7: You're talking with a friend from class during your break. You see someone you want to meet. Your friend knows this person. You want <u>your friend</u> to introduce you. What do you ask your friend?

_____

_____ ***D.** **Beyond the book: Make questions of permission or request that you might ask in these situations: your first day at a new school, your first day on a new job, your first week in a new apartment building. (You may work in small groups.)**

EXAMPLE: Could you please tell me where to register for classes?

PART FOUR / *It/there*; Frequency Words

● Stating Weather Conditions ● Describing Problems with Homesickness

it: with weather	*there*: with weather
Sometimes the word *it* is a "filler." That is, it fills the place of the subject, but it doesn't have real meaning. The filler *it* often occurs in sentences about the weather.	Sometimes the word *there* is a filler with the verb *be* and a noun. However, *there* is not the subject. The noun in the sentence is the subject, and *be* agrees with it.
It's windy. It's a cloudy day. It snows a lot. Is it sunny?	There's a lot of wind. There are clouds. There's a lot of snow. Is there sunshine?

A. **Use *it* and *there* to make affirmative (+) and negative (–) sentences. In each case, use the simple present tense of the underlined verb.**

EXAMPLE: **1.** It's beautiful today, isn't it?

1. _____ / <u>be</u> beautiful today, isn't it?   (+)

2. Oh, yes. In my country, _____ / <u>be</u> a lot of fog at this time of year.   (+)

3. People tell me that _____ / <u>be</u> much fog in this area.   (–)

4. That's true. But _____ / <u>rain</u> a lot.   (+)

5. In some of our big cities, _____ / <u>be</u> a lot of smog.   (+)

6. But _____ / <u>be</u> usually smoggy in the wintertime, is it?   (–)

7. No, not very. <u>Be</u> / _____ / very hot in your area?   (+)

8. Yes, but _____ / <u>be</u> often a thunderstorm in the afternoon,   (++)

and after that _____ / <u>get</u> cooler.

9. <u>Be</u> / _____ / a lot of wind in your area?   (+)

10. No, _____ / <u>be</u> usually much wind, but _____ / <u>be</u>   (–+)
sometimes breezy for a short time in the afternoon.

> ### *there*: with the present continuous tense
>
> You can sometimes the filler *there* with the present continuous tense. The subject comes between the verb *be* and verb-*ing*.
>
> | *be* | **Subject** | **Verb-*ing*** |
> | --- | --- | --- |
> | There are | people | introducing themselves. |
> | Is there | someone | serving punch? |

B. **Look back at the picture on page 11 and then make sentences to answer these questions. Use *there* and the present continuous tense.**

EXAMPLE: 1. Yes, there is a student yawning.

1. Is there anyone yawning? _____

2. Are there people standing in line? _____

_____

3. Is there anyone sitting down? _____

4. Are there people checking the schedule of classes? _____

_____

5. Is there anyone shrugging? _____

Make a question for each answer below.

6. _____
Yes, there's a student walking into Room 107.

7. _____
Yes, there are are people taking the placement test.

8. _____
No, there isn't anyone eating.

9. _____
Yes, there's a woman reading.

10. _____
Yes, there's someone asking for directions.

Frequency Words

Common Frequency Words	Meaning
always	all of the time
usually / generally	most (of) the time
often / frequently	a lot of the time
sometimes / occasionally	now and then / from time to time
seldom[1] / rarely[1]	not often
never[1]	not ever

In statements, these frequency words usually appear before the simple present verb, except for the verb *be*.

> They seldom argue.
> He's never careful with his budget.

In the negative, the frequency words come between the verb *do* and the main verb.

> He doesn't often give speeches.
> They don't always get the classes they want.

In questions, the frequency words usually come after the subject.

> Do they usually have a get-acquainted party?
> Why do you generally take classes in the evening?

The word *ever* is used only in questions and in negative statements. It means "at any time."

> Do you ever take morning classes?
> No, I don't ever take morning classes.

[1] *Seldom, rarely,* and *never* are negative. Don't use them with *not. All of the time* and *most of the time* usually come at the end of a sentence.

From time to time, most of the time, and *now and then* may also come at the beginning.

C. Make sentences from these words.

EXAMPLE: **1.** Do you ever feel homesick?

1. _____
you / ever / feel / do / homesick / ?

2. _____
yes, / often / I / my country and my family / miss / .

3. _____
call you / does / sometimes / your family / ?

4. _____
no, / call / they / never / . / but / all the time / each other / write / we / .

5. _____

do / when you're homesick / what / do / usually / you / ?

6. _____

well, / go to a movie / I / always / .

7. _____

help / does / usually / that / ?

8. _____

no, / it / helps / rarely / , so then / invite / I / some friends / over for dinner / .

_____

always / that / helps / . / seldom / I'm / for a long time / homesick / .

*D. **Beyond the book: Discuss the weather in your hometown and the weather where you are now. Use _it_ and _there_ and be sure to put the frequency words in the correct place in your sentences. (You may work in small groups.)**

EXAMPLE: It's often cold here in the evenings in the summer. In my hometown, it always stays warm.

*E. **Beyond the book: Discuss or write about homesickness. Do you ever get homesick? If so, what do you usually do about it?**

EXAMPLE: I often get homesick. I sometimes call my family when this happens, but the phone calls are expensive, so I usually just go out for coffee with a friend.

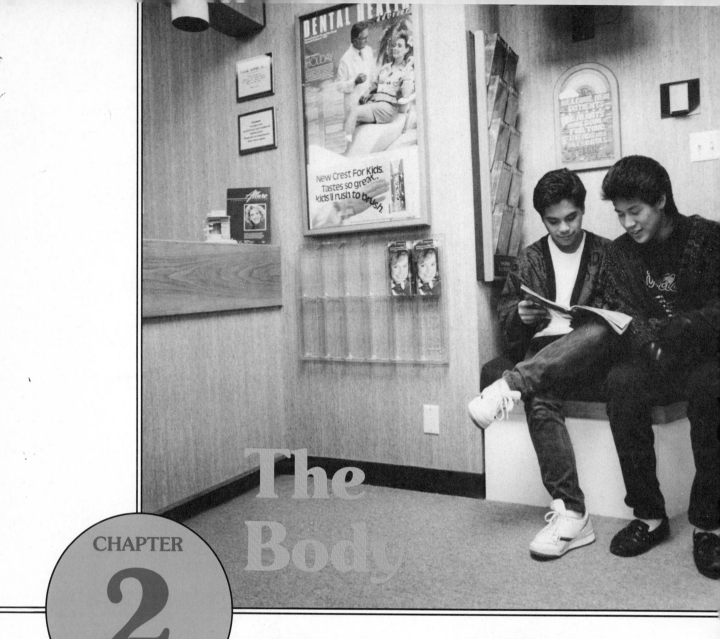

The Body

GRAMMAR:

Nonaction verbs; verbs with
   action and nonaction
   meanings
Simple modals of possibility
   and probability
Simple modals of advice
Causatives

COMPETENCIES:

Discussing nutrition (good
   food vs. "junk food")
Understanding procedures
   in waiting rooms
Discussing disease prevention
   and leading causes of death
Getting immunizations
Discussing dental care
Discussing prenatal care
Giving advice about health
Discussing exercise programs
Reading and comparing food
   labels

How much do you already know? Read the following paragraphs and choose the correct words. Circle your answers.

A lot of people [sit/are sitting] in the waiting room of a neighborhood clinic. They're at this
1.

clinic because it's free, and they [know/are knowing] that they [might not/shouldn't] go to a
2.   3.

private hospital for regular medical care. Most of these people [want/are wanting] to see a doctor.
4.

The others [ought to/must] be their friends or relatives.
5.

When patients walk in, they go to the receptionist first and give her their names. She has them

[fill/to fill] out a form. If they [don't understand/aren't understanding] some questions or words
6.   7.

on this form, they should [ask/to ask] her for help.
8.

One woman is walking into the doctor's office. Her husband [crosses/is crossing] his fingers;
9.

he must [tell/be telling] her "good luck." Another woman is trying to get her little boy [sits/to
10.   11.

sit] down and be quiet, but he [doesn't mind/isn't minding] her. He's asking a man a lot of
12.

questions, but the man [doesn't mind/isn't minding]. He must [like/likes] children.
13.   14.

Wendy Lim is at this clinic because she [has/is having] a stomachache and a skin rash on her
15.

arms and legs. She [thinks/is thinking] that this [might/should] be from some bad food.
16.   17.

Wendy's friend Susan is with her. To pass the time, Susan [looks/is looking] at posters on the
18.

walls that tell how to prevent medical problems. It [looks/is looking] like they [could/ought to]
19.   20.

have a long wait.

score: _____
20

PART ONE   Nonaction Verbs; Verbs with Action and Nonaction Meanings

● Discussing Nutrition (Good Food vs. "Junk Food")

Nonaction Verbs

Don't use the present continuous tense with certain verbs, even if the action is "right now." Instead, use the simple present tense with these nonaction verbs.

Condition	Possession	Emotional or Mental Activity		
consist	belong	appreciate	know	understand
cost	contain	approve	like	want
equal	own	believe	mean	
matter	possess	desire	need	
owe		dislike	prefer	
resemble	**Perception**	doubt	recognize	
	seem	hate	remember	

A. Choose the correct tense for each verb: present continuous or simple present. Everything is happening right now.

EXAMPLES: 1. Ana Lopez is sitting at the kitchen table and
2. writing her grocery list.

Ana Lopez _____ at the kitchen table and _____ her

  1. sit   **2.** write

grocery list. She _____ to plan the week's meals so that they are nutritious. For

  3. try

example, she _____ to buy lots of fresh fruit and vegetables because they

  4. plan

_____ necessary vitamins such as vitamins A and C. Also, Ana _____ that her

5. contain   **6.** know

family _____ protein, but red meat _____ a lot and _____ fat, so Ana

  7. need   **8.** cost   **9.** contain

_____ of buying chicken, fish, or beans instead.

10. think

Ana's kids _____ her to include their favorite foods on her list. They

  11. beg

_____ why she _____ them to have soda pop, candy, and chips.

12. not understand   **13.** not want

Ana _____ to them that soda pop has too much sugar and no vitamins at all.

  14. explain

She _____ for them to drink milk—with vitamin D and calcium—or fruit juice—
    15. prefer

with vitamin C. Her kids _____ that candy does terrible things to their teeth and
            16. not remember

that chips have too much salt. It _____ to her kids that Ana _____ of
          17. seem   **18.** not approve

anything that they _____ . But she just _____ them to be healthy.
        19. like   **20.** want

Verbs with Action and Nonaction Meanings

Some verbs have more than one meaning. In the nonaction meaning, the verb is in the simple present tense. In the action meaning, the verb is in the present continuous tense if the action is happening right now. Here are some of these verbs with their meanings.

Verbs	Nonaction Meaning	Action Meaning
Condition:		
be	He is tall.	He's being very good. (be = behave/act)
fit	The suit fits well.	The tailor is fitting him for a new suit. (fit = measure for; cause to fit or conform)
match	Her shoes match her dress. (match = looks attractive with)	I'm matching this tie with these shirts. (match = try to put together)
weigh	He weighs 150 pounds.	He's weighing himself now. (weigh = put on a scale)
Possession:		
have	I have a typewriter. (have = possess)	I'm having some problems. (have = experience) He's having breakfast. (have = eat/drink) She's having a baby. (have = be pregnant with or give birth to) They're having a party. (have = give)
Perception:		
appear	He appears to be ready. (appear = seem)	She's appearing in a new play. (appear = perform or come into sight)
feel	I feel it's a good idea. (feel = think/believe) He feels relieved. (feel = have an emotion)	I'm feeling better now. (feel = experience an emotion or physical feeling) She's feeling around for the light switch. (feel = touch)
hear	He doesn't hear you. (hear = perceive with the ears)	You'll be hearing from my lawyer. (hear = get a letter or call)
look	You look tired. (look = seem)	He's looking at you. (look = use one's eyes)
see	I see him over there. (see = perceive with the eyes)	The mayor is seeing her now. (see = meet with)
smell	This smells good! (smell = have a smell)	She's smelling every perfume in the store. (smell = sniff)
sound	That sounds like a good idea. (sound = seem) The music sounds loud. (sound = have a sound)	They're sounding the alarm. (sound = cause a sound)
taste	This tastes great! (taste = have a taste) I taste something strange. (taste = perceive a taste)	He's tasting your cake now. (taste = try, sample food)
Emotional/Mental Activity:		
guess	I guess we should start. (guess = suppose)	He's just guessing. (guess = make an estimate)
imagine	I imagine that you're tired. (imagine = guess, think)	You're just imagining things. (imagine = use the imagination)
mean	It means "no." (mean = signify)	I've been meaning to do that. (mean = intend)
mind	I don't mind. (mind = object to)	Who's minding the store? (mind = take care of) The boy is minding his mother. (mind = do what is asked)
think	I think it's too big. (think = believe, have an opinion)	Wait a second. I'm thinking. (think = consider, reflect)

B. Use the chart on page 30 to help you decide if the verbs in the following sentences have the action or nonaction meaning. Then give the present continuous tense for action meanings and the simple present tense for nonaction meanings.

EXAMPLE: **1. a.** These people are having lunch at a fast-food place.

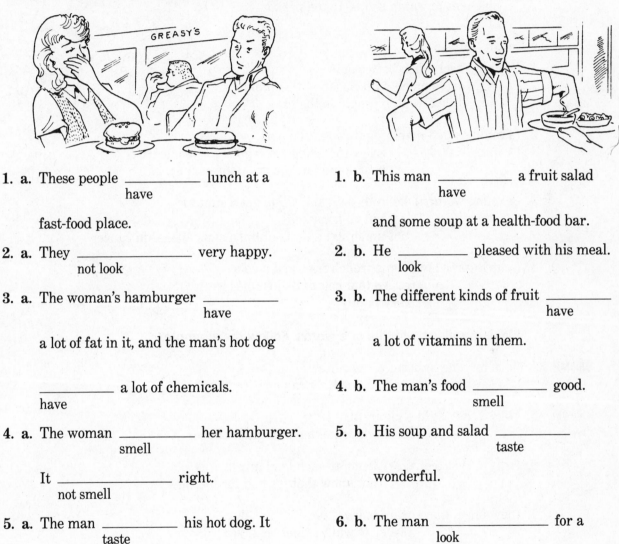

1. a. These people _____ lunch at a
              have

fast-food place.

2. a. They _____ very happy.
              not look

3. a. The woman's hamburger _____
                                      have

a lot of fat in it, and the man's hot dog

_____ a lot of chemicals.
have

4. a. The woman _____ her hamburger.
                       smell

It _____ right.
    not smell

5. a. The man _____ his hot dog. It
                     taste

_____ strange.
taste

6. a. They _____ they want
                 not think

to come back here.

1. b. This man _____ a fruit salad
                      have

and some soup at a health-food bar.

2. b. He _____ pleased with his meal.
             look

3. b. The different kinds of fruit _____
                                         have

a lot of vitamins in them.

4. b. The man's food _____ good.
                           smell

5. b. His soup and salad _____
                               taste

wonderful.

6. b. The man _____ for a
                     look

waitress. He _____ of
                think

ordering something else because

everything _____ so good.
              look

C. **Make sentences with the cue words. Use the present continuous for the underlined verbs with action meanings and the simple present for the underlined verbs with nonaction meanings. Everything is happening right now.**

EXAMPLE: 1. Wendy is feeling much better now.
             She's having lunch with Susan at this moment.
             She likes to watch people in the park.

1. (Wendy) <u>feel</u> much better now
            <u>have</u> lunch with Susan at this moment
            <u>like</u> to watch people in the park

2. (a middle-aged man) <u>jog</u> through the park
                        <u>know</u> that exercise is good for his heart
                        <u>hear</u> some soft music on his earphones

3. (a young woman) <u>lie</u> in the sun and <u>try</u> to get a suntan
                    <u>not put</u> on sunscreen
                    <u>not understand</u> that sunburn can cause skin cancer

4. (a little girl) <u>have</u> some french fries and a cola
                    <u>not realize</u> that cola is bad for her teeth
                    <u>look</u> very happy

Make questions with the cue words. Follow the example.

EXAMPLE: 5. Why is he lighting a cigarette?
             Doesn't he realize that smoking can cause cancer?

5. (why / he) light a cigarette
              not realize that smoking can cause cancer

6. (why / that teenager) listen to such loud music
                         not know that it's bad for his ears

7. (how far / they) walk today
                    prefer to walk rather than jog

8. (how / he) avoid a sunburn
              have a hat

9. (why / she) get candy at the snack bar
               not understand that candy is "junk food"

*D. **Beyond the book: Go to a busy public place, such as a park. Watch the people around you. Discuss or write about the people and activities that you see. What are they doing to keep healthy? What are they doing that's bad for their health?**

EXAMPLE: The man on the park bench is smoking. His cough sounds bad.

PART TWO / Simple Modals of Possibility and Probability

● Understanding Procedures in Waiting Rooms ● Discussing Disease Prevention and Leading Causes of Death

---

Simple Modals of Possibility and Probability

You can express present or future possibility with the modals *may, might,* or *could* and the simple form of the main verb. You can express probability with *must* and the simple form of the verb.

Subject	Modal	(*not*)[1]	Verb
She	may		need a doctor. (= Maybe she needs a doctor.)
He	might	not	understand. (= Maybe he doesn't understand.)
We	could		need some rest. (= Maybe we need some rest.)
They	must		want to buy health insurance. (= Probably they want to buy health insurance.)

You can also use the continuous with these modals.

He might be trying to find a job with health insurance as a benefit.
(= Maybe he is trying to find a job with health insurance as a benefit.)

He must not be feeling well. (= Probably he isn't feeling well.)

[1] may not = maybe not, might not = maybe not
But: couldn't = definitely not ("for sure" not)

Leading Causes of Death in the United States

1900	1985
1. Influenza and pneumonia	1. Heart disease
2. Tuberculosis (T.B.)	2. Cancer
3. Diarrhea and related diseases	3. Stroke
4. Heart disease	4. Accidents
5. Stroke	5. Pneumonia

Leading Causes of Death in the United States and Related Risk Factors, 1985

Cause of Death	Risk Factors
1. Heart disease	Smoking, poor diet, lack of exercise, stress, high blood pressure
2. Cancer	Smoking, poor diet, cancer-causing chemicals in the environment
3. Stroke	Smoking, poor diet, high blood pressure, stress
4. Accidents (excluding motor vehicles)	Alcohol, smoking (fires), drug use
5. Pneumonia	Smoking

A.   **Look at the charts on page 33 and then make sentences that mean the same as the following sentences. Use modals of possibility and probability. (In some cases, there are several correct answers.)**

EXAMPLE: 1. Exercise may (might, could) help to prevent heart disease.

1. Maybe exercise helps to prevent heart disease. = _____

    _____ (might, could)_____

2. Maybe too many people aren't eating right. = _____

    Maybe too many ~~people~~ might not be right

3. T.B. probably isn't a problem in the United States now. = _____

    T.B probably may not be

4. A lot of Americans probably smoke. = _____

    _____ (may might)_____

5. Maybe the American diet is changing. = _____

    could the American diet is changing

6. Maybe a lot of people don't know how to relax. = _____

    _____ may not know to relax.

7. Smoking is probably doing terrible things to people's bodies. = _____

    _____ (maybe) could)_____

8. Maybe some people don't know about the importance of exercise. = _____

    _____ might not know_____

9. Maybe some people are smoking in bed. = _____

    _____ maybe_____

B.

Read the following paragraph and then answer the questions about it. Use modals of possibility and probability in your answers. (Make as many sentences as possible for each question.) Numbers in the paragraph refer to numbered questions below.

[1]A man is in a doctor's waiting room. [2]He's shaking all over and holding his forehead. [3]The receptionist hands him a form. [4]He begins to fill it out, but then he stops writing, goes to the receptionist, points to something on the form, and asks her a question. Then he finishes the form. [5]Another person in the waiting room lights a cigarette. Her hands are shaking slightly. [6]Everyone in the room looks at her and frowns. [7]A man points to a sign on the wall, and she puts out her cigarette. [8]Another woman comes out of the doctor's office. She hands the receptionist a health insurance card and the receptionist takes it. [9]The woman turns to her husband and makes an "O" with her thumb and first finger. [10]Her husband smiles and pats her on the shoulder.

EXAMPLE: **1.** He might be sick. He could be waiting for the doctor. He may work there.

1. Why is the man in the doctor's waiting room? _He shoking all over and holding his forehead._

2. What's wrong with him? _____

3. What is this form? _He fill it out your medical form._

4. What is he asking her? _He asks her a question_

5. How does this woman feel? _her hands are shoking slightly_

6. Why are the other people frowning? _Because the man_

7. What does the sign say? _might be "no smoking area"_

8. Does the woman's health insurance plan cover office visits? _____

9. What is she telling her husband with her body language? _she turны to her husband and make an "O" with her thumb and first finger_

10. Why does he pat her on the back? _May be she's okay or healthly_

PART THREE / Simple Modals of Advice

● Getting Immunizations ● Discussing Dental Care ● Discussing Prenatal Care
● Giving Advice about Health

Simple Modals of Advice

You can express advice with *should* or *ought to* and the simple form of the main verb. The meaning is present or future. You can also express the continuous with *should* or *ought to*.

> You should fill out the medical form completely.
> He shouldn't[1] be afraid to ask the doctor questions.
> She ought to be exercising.

You can express strong advice or a warning with *had better*.

> You had better learn to relax.
> He had better not smoke.

[1] Use *shouldn't* in the negative; *ought not to* is uncommon.

A. Complete the sentences with modals of advice. Follow the example.

EXAMPLE: **1. a:** What should I do to quit smoking?
           b: You ought to go to a program at the American Lung Association.

1. a: What ___should___ I do to quit smoking?

   b: You ___ought to___ go to a program at the American Lung Association.

2. a: What ___should___ I do to get over this flu?

   b: You ___had better___ stay in bed, drink liquids, take aspirin, and keep warm.

3. a: When ___should___ my child have her first appointment with a dentist?

   b: She ___ought to___ see a dentist when she's about three.

   She ___must___ learn not to be afraid of dentists.

4. a: How much salt _should_ we have in our diet?

   b: You _should_ consume no more than eight grams a day.

5. a: How _should_ we cut down on salt?

   b: You _must_ be careful to read the labels on packaged food.

      You _might_ not add extra salt to fresh food.

6. a: How much _ought_ I exercise?

   b: You _must_ get twenty minutes of very active exercise three times a week.

      You _ought_ not start an exercise program before a doctor checks you.

7. a: How _____ we decide on a good health insurance program?

   b: You _____ call several insurance companies and ask them to send you information.

      You _____ not buy health insurance before you compare medical plans.

8. a: How _____ I choose a good podiatrist for the problem with my foot?

   b: You _____ ask your family doctor to suggest one.

      You _____ not just pick one from the phone book.

B. **Look at the three charts that follow. With a partner, make as many questions and answers as possible. Use the information on the charts and *should(n't)*, *ought to*, and *had better*.**

EXAMPLE: **a:** At what age should a baby have his first shots?

b: He ought to have a DPT shot at two months.

PROTECT YOUR CHILDREN WITH IMMUNIZATION!

Don't take chances with your child's health!

	DPT	Polio	Mumps/ Rubella/ Measles	T.B. Test	Hib	Tetanus/ Diphtheria
2 months	X	X				
4 months	X	X				
6 months	X					
1 year				X		
15 months			X			
1-1/2 yrs	X	X				
2-6 yrs					X	
14-16 yrs						X

DENTAL CARE

See your dentist twice a year.
Brush after every meal.
Use dental floss daily.
Use mouthwash with fluoride.
Brush "up and down"—not "across."

PREGNANT?
Protect your unborn child!

Don't smoke.
Don't drink alcohol.
Avoid caffeine.
Increase your calcium to 1,200 mg. per day.
Drink 6–8 glasses of liquids a day.
Don't skip meals; eat 3 meals a day.
Eat healthful snacks.
See your obstetrician once a month.

C. Give advice in the following situations. (There are several possible answers for each situation.)

EXAMPLE: **Situation 1:** He ought to go to a free clinic. He shouldn't go to a hospital.

Situation 1: A person is new to this country. He doesn't have a job yet, so he doesn't have much money. He also doesn't have health insurance. He's having problems with his back.

_____

_____

Situation 2: A woman has an appointment with her doctor at 11:15. She arrived at the doctor's office at 11:10. Now it's 11:50, and she's still waiting.

she must ask a Receptionist

she shouldn't waiting longer

Situation 3: A man and woman are afraid that their teenage son might be taking drugs.

they must ask him about it

they should have a meeting

Situation 4: A woman is taking her four-year-old child to the dentist for the first time. The child is afraid.

she should be explain

she must be encourage go to the dentist

Situation 5: You're in the doctor's examining room. He's telling you to take a certain medicine, but you don't know why because you don't really understand what's wrong with you. Also, you're afraid that the medicine might have harmful side effects.

_____

_____

Situation 6: A friend of yours is new to this country. She seems depressed—not happy at all. She stays home most of the time and sleeps a lot. She doesn't seem sick, but she's tired all the time.

_____

_____

PART FOUR / Causatives

● Discussing Exercise Programs ● Reading and Comparing Food Labels

---

Causatives

Certain verbs—causatives—show that someone is causing another person to do something. Four common causatives are *let, make, have,* and *get.*

     let = permit or allow
     make = order, force, give someone no choice (the subject has power to
                  cause the action)
     have = request, ask, or pay someone to do something
     get = persuade, convince

	Subject	Causative	Object	Verb	
	She	lets	him	eat	a lot of fruit.
Does	she	make	them	take	vitamin pills?
	He	has	us	drink	nonfat milk.
How do	you	get	him	to exercise?	

 A. **Make new sentences. Use causatives instead of the underlined words. Do not change the meanings of the sentences.**

EXAMPLE: 1. My friend George, who is helping me lose weight, makes me exercise every other day.

1. My friend George, who is helping me lose weight, <u>forces me to exercise</u> every other day.

2. He always <u>asks me to warm up</u> with slow, easy exercises.

3. Then he <u>persuades me to move</u> faster and work harder.

4. He never <u>permits me to give up</u>, but he also doesn't <u>force</u> me to exercise too hard.

5. He <u>asks me to walk fast</u> for several miles a day, and he <u>forces me to wear</u> good, comfortable shoes.

6. These days, he's also <u>persuading me to watch</u> my diet. For example, he's <u>asking me to eat</u> a healthful breakfast every day.

7. He's also <u>forcing me to drink</u> a lot of water, and he isn't <u>permitting me to drink</u> any soft drinks.

8. I'm <u>asking my wife to cook</u> with very little oil, salt, or sugar these days. I'm <u>asking her to use</u> spices instead.

9. She and George are actually <u>persuading me to enjoy</u> vegetables, fruit, whole-grain cereal, and meat without fat.

10. Because of this good influence, I'm also trying to <u>persuade my kids to exercise</u> more.

11. Sometimes I <u>persuade them to come</u> for a long walk with me in the evening.

12. I don't want to <u>permit them to get</u> as out of shape as I am.

B.

Make questions and answers with words from the lists below. You might need to change the forms of the verbs. Make both affirmative and negative sentences.

EXAMPLE: a: Do you have your kids take vitamin pills?
b: Yes, I have them take one multiple vitamin pill every day, but I don't let them take more than that.

Subject	Causative	Object	Verb
you	let	you/yourself	eat a lot of vegetables
your mother	make	your kids	eat candy
your parents	have	your brother	go to the dentist twice a year
your wife	get	your sister	help with the cooking
your husband		your husband	do the grocery shopping
your friends		your friends	exercise (with you/him/her/them)
			take vitamin pills
			drink a lot of milk
			eat breakfast

*C.   **Beyond the book: Bring labels to class from empty boxes of cereal, cans of various foods, and packages of frozen food. Compare the vitamins, calories, fat, and sodium (salt) in these. Which are good for you? Which have a lot of salt or fat? Why do you have your family eat certain foods? What foods are difficult to get your family to eat? What foods do you sometimes let your family (or yourself) eat that are "junk food"? Is it possible to make yourself eat only healthful foods? (You may work with a partner or in small groups to discuss these questions.)**

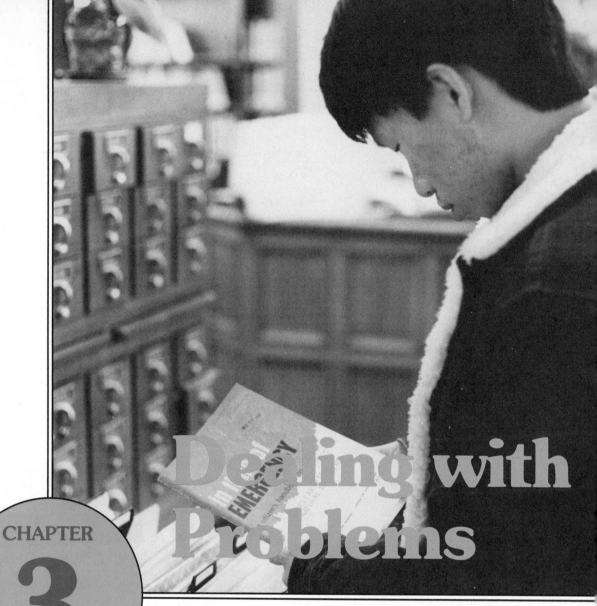

Dealing with Problems

CHAPTER

3

GRAMMAR:
The simple past tense:
  statements
The simple past tense:
  questions
The past continuous tense
Used to/Would

COMPETENCIES:
Preventing break-ins
Describing accidents
Taking care of oneself and
  others in earthquakes,
  blackouts, hurricanes,
  and fires

How much do you already know? **Read the following story and choose the correct words. Circle your answers.**

Freddy [had / was having] a lot of problems when he first arrived in the United States.
1.

Everything [seemed / was seeming] very strange to him. For example, he [not understood / didn't
2.   3.

understand] the American idea that "Time is money." He lost the chance to get several different

jobs because he [use to / used to] arrive late for job interviews.
4.

One day, while he [drove / was driving] to another job interview, a police officer [stopped / was
5.   6.

stopping] him because his car had a broken taillight. The officer checked Freddy's driver's license

and registration. "[You knew / Did you know] that your car registration [expired / was expiring]
7.   8.

last month?" the officer asked. Freddy sadly shook his head. As the officer [wrote / was writing]
9.

out a ticket, Freddy suddenly [remembered / was remembering] his job interview and [realized /
10.   11.

was realizing] that he was late again. He sighed. Life [would be / used to be] easier when he was
12.

back in his country. He didn't [use to / used to] have so many problems.
13.

Another day, as he [unlocked / was unlocking] his apartment door, Freddy [heard / was
14.   15.

hearing] a noise inside. Although it was very dangerous and not at all smart to do so, he rushed in

and saw two kids who [went / were going] out the window with his portable T.V. He ran toward
16.

the window but tripped and [fell / was falling] over a cushion that [lay / was lying] on the floor.
17.   18.

"At least," he thought later, "my household insurance will pay for a new T.V." But when he

[called / was calling] his insurance agent, she told him, "Sorry. You [didn't paid / didn't pay] your
19.   20.

premium on time, so you don't have any insurance coverage."

score: _____

20

PART ONE / The Simple Past Tense: Statements

● Preventing Break-ins

The Simple Past Tense: Statements

Affirmative (regular)[1]

Subject	Verb-*ed*
He	worried about crime.
They	wanted a safer neighborhood.

Negative (regular and irregular)

Subject	*didn't*	Verb
Freddy	didn't	live in a safe neighborhood.
He	didn't	know most of his neighbors.

Affirmative (irregular)[2]

Subject	Verb
People	came at 7:00.
He	found a place to meet.

You can use the simple past tense for a finished action that began and ended in the past. Some common expressions are:

yesterday	last year
at 1:45	two days ago
last week	a while ago
last weekend	when he was a child
last month	in 1980

[1]The past forms of *be* are *was* (for *I, he, she, it*) and *were* (for *you, we,* and *they*). Negative forms are *wasn't* and *weren't.*

[2]There is no one rule that covers all irregular verbs. These verbs are in several groups. (See Appendix B on page 180.)

A. After the break-in and burglary of Freddy's apartment, he and a neighbor, Susana, decided to start a Neighborhood Watch program to help prevent crime in their area. What did they do to get the program started? Use the following words to make affirmative (+) and negative (–) sentences in the simple past tense.

EXAMPLE: 1. They planned a date and time for a meeting of neighbors.

1. They / <u>plan</u> a date and time for a meeting of neighbors.   (+)

2. They / <u>choose</u> a place for the meeting.   (+)

3. Freddy / <u>call</u> the police department and / <u>ask</u> for a police officer to come to the meeting.   (++)

4. They both / <u>go</u> from door to door and / <u>invite</u> everyone.   (++)

5. They / <u>make</u> a list of everyone who / <u>accept</u>.   (++)

6. They / <u>want</u> the meeting to be a success, so they / <u>forget</u> to call and remind everyone the day before the meeting.   (+ –)

7. On the day of the meeting, Freddy / <u>want</u> to waste any time, so he / <u>get</u> up early.   (– +)

8. Susana / <u>bring</u> over some borrowed folding chairs and / <u>set</u> them up.   (++)

9. They / <u>have</u> much space, so they / <u>move</u> the furniture around.   (– +)

10. Freddy / <u>make</u> some coffee, and Susana / <u>buy</u> some doughnuts.   (++)

11. Then they / <u>sit</u> down and / <u>wait</u> for people to arrive.   (++)

B. At the meeting, what did (and didn't) the policeman do? Make affirmative (+) and negative (–) sentences with the following words. Use the simple past tense.

EXAMPLE: He got there a few minutes early.

1. get there a few minutes early   (+)

_____

2. set up a movie projector   (+)

_____

3. show a short film   (+)

_____

4. talk during the film   (–)

_____

5. explain something about crime prevention   (+)

_____

6. speak too fast   (–)

_____

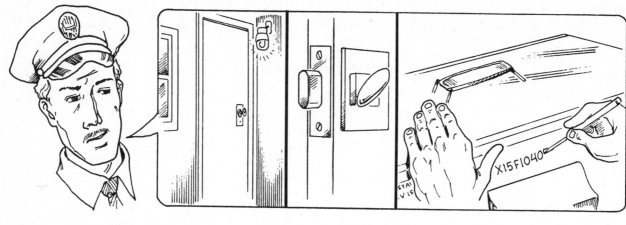

7. tell people about the importance of outdoor lights   (+)

_____

8. say that they needed dead-bolt locks on their doors   (+)

_____

9. suggest marking their T.V.s and stereos with a special number   (+)

_____

10. leave right away   (–)

_____

11. answer all their questions   (+)

_____

12. give everyone Neighborhood Watch decals for their windows   (+)

_____

C.   Complete the following sentences with the simple past tense of the verbs.

EXAMPLE: 1. In the weeks after their first Neighborhood Watch meeting, the neighbors began to change their habits.

In the weeks after their first Neighborhood Watch meeting, the neighbors _____ to

                                                     1. begin

change their habits. They _____ dead-bolt locks and always _____ their doors when

                      2. buy   **3. lock**

they _____ the house, even for a few minutes. They also _____ special locks for their

     4. leave   **5. find**

windows and _____ sure that it _____ possible to open the bars on bedroom windows

           6. make   **7. be**

in case of fire. They _____ their driver's license numbers or other I.D. numbers on the back

         8. put

of their T.V.s and stereos with a special tool that they _____ from the police department.
                                                           9. borrow

They _____ their expensive jewelry and other valuables and _____ them in a bank
        10. take   11. put

safety deposit box. Most of the people _____ timers and _____ them to one or two
                                          12. get   13. attach

inside lights so that the lights _____ on when they _____ home.
                                  14. come   15. not be

Most importantly, the neighbors _____ to know each other and _____ an eye on
                                  16. get   17. keep

each other's homes. Once, when someone _____ into the house across the street, Susana
                                          18. break

_____ him. She _____ the police and _____ down the license plate number of
19. see   20. call   21. write

the person's car. When the thief _____ the police siren, he _____ through a back door
                                  22. hear   23. flee

and _____ behind the garage, but he _____ to escape. The police _____
    24. hide   25. not manage   26. catch

him and _____ him away to the police car.
         27. lead

Once, Susana _____ away on a short vacation and _____ to stop her mail and
              28. go   29. forget

newspaper delivery, so Freddy _____ her mail for her and _____ the
                               30. collect   31. not let

newspapers pile up on her doorstep.

In this way, as the neighbors _____ each other, crime _____ less of a problem in
                               32. help   33. become

the area. Criminals _____ to be caught, so they _____ off to other neighborhoods
                     34. not want   35. go

where people _____ Neighborhood Watch Programs. Of course, crime _____
             36. not have   37. not go

away completely, but people _____ safer as the number of break-ins _____ .
                             38. feel   39. go down

*D.   **Beyond the book: Discuss or write about crime and crime prevention. Did anyone
           ever break into your home or the home of a friend or relative? If so, how did they
           get in? What did they take? Was crime a problem in your country? What did
           people do to prevent it?**

PART TWO / The Simple Past Tense: Questions

● Describing Accidents

The Simple Past Tense: Questions

There is only *one* verb in the question if the important part of the answer is the *subject*. The verb in the question is in the simple past tense.

Question Word (Subject)	Verb ?
What	happened?
(Answer: Something terrible	happened.)
Who	stole her car?
(Answer: That man	stole it.)

There are *two* verbs in the question (*did* and the simple form of the main verb) if the important part of the answer is the verb, object, place, time, reason, or anything except the subject. The subject comes between the two verbs in the question.

Question Word	*did*	Subject	Verb ?
When	did	the robbery	happen?
(Answer:		It	happened yesterday.)
	Did	they	take anything?
(Answer: Yes,		they	took our stereo.)

In questions where the verb is *be*, don't use *did*. Instead, the word order is subject-verb if the important part of the answer is the subject.

Question Word (Subject)	*be* ?
Who	was a witness to the accident?
(Answer: Those people	were witnesses.)

The word order is verb-subject if the important part of the answer is *not* the subject.

Question Word	*be*	Subject
Where	were	they?
(Answer:		They were on the corner.)
	Was	anyone hurt?
(Answer: Yes,		a man was hurt.)

A. Freddy saw a traffic accident one day and realized that someone was hurt. He ran to a public phone and called 911 for an ambulance and the police. Make questions about Freddy's experience. Use the simple past tense. Don't use any of the underlined words in your questions.

EXAMPLE: 1. Where did the accident happen?

1. _____
The accident happened <u>at the corner of 5th and Main</u>.

2. _____
It occurred <u>just a minute ago</u>.

3. _____
<u>Yes</u>, someone got hurt.

4. _____
<u>Two</u> cars were involved.

5. _____
<u>Yes</u>, I saw the accident.

6. _____
<u>The driver of the blue car</u> caused it.

7. _____
He <u>drove through a red light and crashed into the other car</u>.

8. _____
<u>Nobody</u> else saw it.

9. _____

I ran the red light <u>because I didn't see it.</u>

10. _____

<u>No,</u> I wasn't drunk.

11. _____

I didn't renew my driver's license <u>because I forgot.</u>

12. _____

They took me <u>to Huntington Hospital.</u>

13. _____

They operated on me <u>yesterday.</u>

14. _____

<u>No,</u> the person who hit me didn't have auto insurance.

15. _____

<u>Yes,</u> I remembered to pay my auto insurance on time, <u>thank goodness.</u>

16. _____

<u>Yes, of course</u> I had insurance coverage for uninsured motorists.

B. Look at the following newspaper article about a different kind of accident. What questions did the reporter ask before he wrote the article? Make questions using as many question words in the list below as possible.

EXAMPLE: When did the fire break out?

Two Die in Apartment Fire

Fire broke out last night on the second floor of the Claxton Arms Apartments. The fire quickly spread to the first and third floors. Thirty-two people escaped unhurt after smoke detectors woke them. However, two people on the first floor died of smoke inhalation; the security bars on their bedroom window did not open from inside the room.

Fire fighters arrived at 11:56 and had the fire under control by 12:25. The homeless thirty-two people spent the night at a nearby motel, where the Red Cross brought them food and clothing.

what	how	why	how long	what time
where	who	when	how many	

1. _____

2. _____

3. _____

4. _____

5. _____

6. _____

 C. Beyond the book: With a partner, ask and answer questions about accidents. Were you ever in a car accident or fire here or in your country? Did you ever see one? What caused it? What happened? Was anyone hurt? Who helped people afterwards?

EXAMPLE: a. Were you ever in an accident?
             b: Yes, I was in a car accident once when I was a child.

PART THREE / The Past Continuous Tense

● Taking Care of Oneself and Others in Earthquakes and Blackouts

---

The Past Continuous Tense: Statements

Subject	be (not)	Verb-ing
I	was	waiting to renew my license.
You	were	standing in line.
Freddy	was	worrying about his ticket.
She	was	filling out a form.
They	were	taking the driving test.

You can use the past continuous tense for an action in progress at a specific time in the past.

> They were driving to work at 8:30. (They were driving before 8:30, at 8:30, and probably after 8:30.)

You can also use the past continuous tense for two past actions that happened at the same time. In this case, the emphasis is on the duration of each action; you usually need the word *while* or *as*.

> He <u>was studying</u> the driving laws as he <u>was standing</u> in line at the department of motor vehicles.

You can also use the past continuous tense for a past action that was in progress when another action happened.

> He <u>was standing</u> in line at the department of motor vehicles when <u>tapped</u>[1] him on the shoulder.

Don't use the past continuous tense with nonaction verbs. Instead, use the simple past tense. For lists of nonaction verbs, see pages 28 and 30.

[1] Use the simple past tense for the shorter of the two actions that happen at the same time.

A. Bob Brown is a workaholic; that is, he works a lot and is always busy. He hates to waste time, so he often does several things at the same time. Make affirmative (+) and negative (–) sentences about things that he did during one day last year. In each sentence, use the simple past tense for the first underlined verb and the past continuous tense for the second and third underlined verb.

EXAMPLE: 1. Bob planned his next day's schedule as he was falling asleep at night.

1. Bob / <u>plan</u> his next day's schedule as he / <u>fall</u> asleep at night.   (++)

2. In the morning, he / <u>read</u> the newspaper while he / <u>have</u> breakfast.   (++)

3. He / <u>listen</u> to news on the car radio as he / <u>drive</u> to work.   (++)

4. He / figure out his budget while he and the other employees / wait   (++)

for a meeting to begin.

5. He / discuss business with his coworkers while they / have lunch.   (++)

6. He / think about his future in the few minutes when he / do anything.   (+–)

7. After work, he / study a business magazine as he / stand in line at   (++)

the department of motor vehicles.

8. He / realize that someone / try to ask him a question because he /   (–++)

concentrate on his magazine.

The Past Continuous Tense: Questions

Question Word (Subject)	be (not)	Verb-ing ?
Who	was	taking the driving test?
(Answer: A woman	was	taking it.)

Question Word	be (not)	Subject	Verb-ing ?
Why	was	he	waiting?
(Answer:		He	was waiting to pay a ticket.)

B. There was a blackout while Bob Brown and Freddy Xenos were at the department of motor vehicles; that is, the electricity suddenly went out for a large part of the city. What were these people doing when the lights went out? Make questions and answers with the cue words. Use the simple past and past continuous tenses. Follow the example.

EXAMPLE: 1. What was Freddy doing when the lights went out?
            He was trying to renew his car registration.

1. (Freddy) the lights go out
          try to renew his car registration

2. (Bob Brown) the electric power go off
              stand in line at the department of motor vehicles

3. (the woman behind Bob) the lights go out
                    ask him for the time

4. (Bob Brown) the woman ask him for the time
            read a business magazine

5. (the secretaries) the electricity go off
                type drivers' licenses

6. (a DMV employee) the lights go out
                give a vision test

7. (several people) the blackout occur
                take the written test

8. (the driving examiner) the traffic signals stop working
                    give a driving test

9. (the woman) the traffic signal go out
            try to make a left-hand turn

10. (a police officer) the electric power go off
                direct traffic

11. (some pedestrians) the traffic signals stop working
                  cross the street

_____ **C.** **In the following story, Freddy is speaking. Read the story and choose the correct tense for each verb. Use the simple past or past continuous tense.**

EXAMPLES: **1.** For my first vacation in this country, I <u>took</u> a bus **2.** and <u>went</u> to visit my cousins in a small town in California.

For my first vacation in this country, I _____ a bus and _____ to visit my cousins
                                          1. take   **2.** go

in California. When my cousin George _____ to invite me, I _____ pretty homesick
                                        3. call   **4.** feel

and depressed, so it was good to hear from him.

On my third day at George's home, we _____ a lazy Saturday evening in the back yard
                                        5. spend

when suddenly it _____—an earthquake. I _____ on the patio and _____
                   6. happen   **7.** sit   **8.** talk

with George when the earthquake _____. We _____ to an open area, away from
                                   9. strike   **10.** run

buildings and power lines. In the house my aunt _____ ice cubes out of the freezer
                                                   11. take

when she _____ the house begin to shake. She immediately _____ the freezer door,
           12. feel   **13.** shut

_____ under the kitchen table, and _____ on to the table legs. My other cousin
14. get   **15.** hold

_____ a record on the stereo when suddenly the needle _____ across the
16. put   **17.** slide

record and the room _____ to shake. She quickly _____ to the inside wall, away from
                       18. begin   **19.** go

the window, and _____ toward the wall. The ground _____ for only about fifteen
                  20. turn   **21.** shake

seconds. When it _____ over, we _____ for injuries; everyone was okay. But we
                   22. be   **23.** check

_____ that dishes _____ all over the dining room. We had to shut off the
24. see   **25.** lie

gas because we could smell that it _____. When my uncle _____ home, we
                                     26. leak   **27.** get

_____ up broken glass and _____ stories about other disasters. We all _____
28. sweep   **29.** exchange   **30.** decide

not to write to my parents about this earthquake because we _____ them to worry.
                                                              31. not want

PART FOUR / *Used to/would*

● Taking Care of Oneself and Others in Hurricanes and Fires

Use *used to* for a repeated action or a habit in the past. It isn't still happening.
Use *would* in the same way as *used to*. However, it isn't as common.

Affirmative Statements

used to	*would*
I used to worry a lot.	I would worry a lot.
He often used to carry a flashlight.[1]	He would often carry a flashlight.[1]

Negative Statements

We didn't use to plan ahead.	We wouldn't plan ahead.

Questions

What did you use to do?	What would you do?
Didn't you use to worry?	Wouldn't you worry?

[1] Frequency adverbs (*often, always*, etc.) come before *used to* and between *would* and the verb.

Don't use *would* for a past situation. Instead, use *used to*: It used to be a problem.

 A. **Freddy and his cousins are cleaning up after an earthquake hit. Make a question for each answer below. Use *used to* or *would*. Don't use any underlined words in your questions.**

EXAMPLE: 1. Did you use to have earthquakes back home, Freddy?

1. _____, Freddy?
   No, we didn't use to have earthquakes back home. But we had hurricanes.

2. _____
   These hurricanes would hit two to three times a year.

3. _____
   Well, they used to be a problem because my family lived near the ocean.

4. _____

We used to <u>cover the windows with boards</u> just before the hurricane hit.

5. _____

<u>The radio</u> used to warn us ahead of time.

6. _____

After we boarded up the windows, we would <u>move the furniture upstairs and then</u> <u>get in the car and drive away from the ocean.</u>

7. _____

<u>No,</u> I didn't use to be scared. <u>When I was a kid, I thought hurricanes were exciting.</u>

8. _____

If we were at school, they used to <u>have our parents get us.</u>

 B. **When George was in high school, they used to have fire drills every other month. Each classroom had a list of rules like the ones below, and everyone had to follow these rules during the fire drills. What did the students use to do? Make statements with the phrases on the list. Use *used to* and *would*.**

EXAMPLE: They used to leave the room quietly.

> ### When the fire bell rings:
>
> Leave the room quietly.
> Take your valuables with you.
> Don't talk.
> Stay with your class.
> Don't push each other.
> Walk outside.
> Wait there for the "all clear" bell.
> Return to class.

*C. **Beyond the book: In small groups, discuss hurricanes, fires, and other disasters. When you were a child, what kind of disasters used to be a problem in your area? How did people use to prepare for them?**

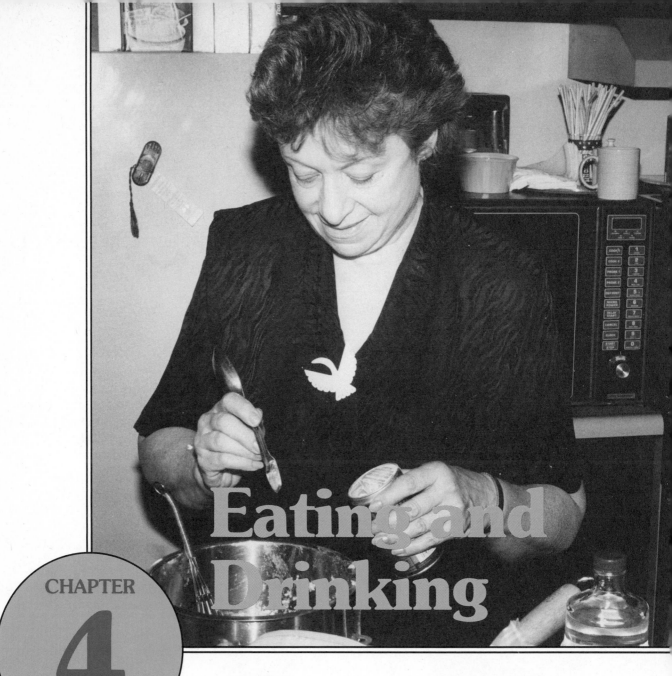

CHAPTER

4

Eating and Drinking

GRAMMAR:
The future: *will* and *be going to*
The future continuous tense: statements and questions
The conditional (future possible)
Two-word verbs: inseparable and separable

COMPETENCIES:
Planning a potluck party
Explaining a recipe
Reading menus
Avoiding food poisoning

How much do you already know? Read the following letters from a newspaper column and choose the correct words. Circle your answers.

Ask Etty Anything

Dear Etty Kit,

Several of us [will throw / are going to throw] a
1.
surprise party for our friend, Freddy, who just got a

job in a restaurant. We don't want to [put off it / put it
2.
off] because we want to celebrate his new job while it's

still new, but we want to do everything right.

We have several questions for you. How can we

throw a wonderful party if we [don't have / won't
3.
have] a lot of money for food and beverages? How

should we invite people? Should we send invitations to

everyone or [call up them / call them up]? [Will you
4.   5.
help / Are you going to help] us?

> Sincerely,
>
> The ESL Group

Dear Group,

Of course I [will help / am going to help]! First,
6.
it's not necessary to send out invitations, except for

formal parties, but if you [decide / will decide] to send
7.
invitations, be sure to write R.S.V.P. in the bottom

Respond.

corner. This tells people to call and answer your

invitation. Then, when you [hear from them / hear
8.
them from], you'll know how many people will

probably [show up / show off] and if anyone wants to
9.
bring a friend along. Also, for an informal party, if you

[write / will write] B.Y.O.B. on the invitations, each
10.

Bring your own Bottle

person [brings / will bring] his or her own bottle of
11.
wine or other alcoholic beverage.

Another good idea for a casual party is to have a

potluck meal. If each guest [brings / will bring] one
12.
dish—either an appetizer, salad, main dish, or

dessert—you'll have a wonderful variety of food, but

nobody [will cook / will be cooking] all week long
13.
before the party.

You need to plan ahead. [Will you have / Are you
14.
going to have] music? [Will you play / Are you going
15.
to play] games? [Figure on / Figure out] everything
16.
that you need to do, and ask each person to [pick out /
17.
pick on] one job to do. Also, let guests at the party help

you if they offer to; it often makes people more

comfortable when they can help.

One more thing. Your guests [are going to bring /
18.
will be bringing] various dishes to your potluck all

evening long; to avoid food poisoning, make sure that

everything is either cold or hot—not warm. And be

sure to [put off / put away] all leftovers immediately—
19.
in the refrigerator.

Good luck with the party. I'm sure that your

friend Freddy [will appreciate / will be appreciating]
20.
your kindness.

> Yours,
>
> Etty

score: _____

20

PART ONE / The Future: *will* and *be going to*

● Planning a Potluck Party ● Explaining a Recipe

Statements

will		
Subject	*will (not)*	Verb
I	will[1]	invite her.
Freddy	won't	be unhappy.
They	will	have fun.

be going to			
Subject	*be (not)*	*going to*	Verb
I	am[2]	going to	invite her.
Freddy	isn't	going to	be unhappy.
They	are	going to	have fun.

You can use *will* + Verb for a future action in these ways:

1. prediction
   He'll be surprised.   =

2. inevitability
   It'll be a lot of work.   =

3. refusal (negative)
   They won't come.   =

4. promise
   I'll bring her.

5. volunteered action
   We'll make a salad.

You can use *be going to* + Verb for a future action in these ways:

1. prediction
   He's going to be surprised.

2. inevitability
   It's going to be a lot of work.

3. refusal (negative)
   They aren't going to come.

4. plan
   I'm going to invite him.

Will (instead of *be going to*) is common with the words *maybe* and *probably*.

[1] Contractions are common with pronouns: *I'll, you'll, he'll, she'll, it'll, we'll, they'll.*

[2] Contractions are common with pronouns: *I'm, you're, he's, she's, it's, we're, they're.*

Questions

will			
Question Word (Subject)		*will*	Verb ?
What		will	happen?
Who		will	be there?

be going to			
Question Word (Subject)		*be going to*	Verb ?
What		is going to	happen?
Who		is going to	be there?

Question Word	*will (not)*	Subject	Verb ?
	Won't	you	come?
What time	will	it	begin?

Question Word	*be (not)*	Subject	*going to*	Verb ?
	Aren't	you	going to	come?
What time	is	it	going to	begin?

A.

Look at the following invitation for Freddy's party. Use *be going to* to make questions and answers about plans for the party.

EXAMPLES:
a. What kind of party is it going to be?
b: It's going to be a surprise party.

> **It's a Surprise Party for Freddy!**
>
> **Day:** Saturday   **Don't bring a gift.**
>
> **Date:** May 7   **Bring a potluck dish!**
>
> **Time:** 8:00
>
> **Place:** 822 Oak Road   R.S.V.P.
>
> **Dress:** casual   555-9876

1. a. ___What a Date is the party? Frudy___
   b. ___its in may 7___
2. a. ___what time?___
   b. ___at 8:00 o'clock.___
3. a. ___where is?___
   b. ___at 822 Oak Road___
4. a. ___what kind of dress are they wearing?___
   b. ___casual dress___
5. a. ___each person have to bring gift?___
   b. ___No, don't bring a gift___
6. a. ___what have to bring?___
   b. ___you have bring a potluck dish___
7. a. ___what is the telephone number?___
   b. ___is 555-9876___
8. a. _____
   b. _____

B. **Make predictions about what is going to happen on the day of the party. Use *will* and *be going to* and the phrases under the picture. Follow the examples.**

EXAMPLES: Francisco is going to answer the phone.

He'll check off names on the guest list.

do the vacuuming
hang the decorations
fix a salad
answer the phone
check off names
put the potato salad in
   the refrigerator

tear down the decorations
have trouble hearing
wash the vegetables
chop the vegetables
toss the salad
boil the eggs

1. Etsuko is going to do the vacuuming
2. Junichiro is will hang the decorations
3. Khalid will fix a salad
4. Francisco will answer the phone
5. Francisco is going to check off names.
6.
7.
8. Minh will wash the vegetables
9. Wendy will chop the vegetables.
10. Ana Maria will boil the eggs.

C.

Make questions about the picture in B. Use *will* and *be going to* in the questions, but don't use the underlined words.

EXAMPLE: **1.** Who will be in charge of the guest list?

1. _____?
Francisco will be in charge of the guest list.

2. *What is Francisco going to do?* ?
He's going to help Etsuko with the cleaning a little later.

3. *where is junichiro going to hang decorations?* ?
Junichiro is going to hang decorations in the living room.

4. *is junichiro will be angry o the cat?* ?
Yes, he'll be a little angry at the cat.

5. *what are going to do Kolihaud Wendy.* ?
They're going to fix two salads.

when will they
6. *when are they going to buy Mirch and Ano florio.* ?
They're going to buy the vegetables early that morning.

where
7. *what are they going to keep the potato salad until the party* ?
They're going to keep the potato salad in the refrigerator until the party.

8. *why are they going to be very careful about potato salad* ?
They'll be very careful about the potato salad because it has mayonnaise in it.

D.

Make questions and answers with the cue words. Use *be going to* and *will*. Follow the example.

EXAMPLE: **1. a.** Is Francisco going to call each guest?
        b. No, he isn't. They'll contact him.

1. a. (Francisco) call each guest
   b. (they) contact him   *He isn't. they contact him*

2. a. (the hosts) fix the whole meal *they*
   b. (each guest) bring a dish   *No won't 1 each guest will bring a dish*

3. a. (they) have only American food
   b. (they) have a variety of international food   *will they have*
                                                       No they won't

4. a. *invitados* (the guests) bring gifts for the hosts   *no* they won't, each person will bring

   b. *dueños* (each person) bring food for the meal instead

5. a. (the hosts) serve dinner to everyone   will the host.

   b. (each person) serve himself or herself   no, they won't. each person serve himself

6. a. (they) put all the food on the table right away

   b. (they) keep some of it in the refrigerator and some in the oven

7. a. (people) send thank-you notes after the party

   b. (they) not need to because it's an informal party

---

*E. *was ello!* **Beyond the book: Plan a potluck party for your class. Use *be going to* to ask and answer questions about plans. What are you going to need? Where are you going to have the party? Are you going to have music and games? Use *will* when you volunteer to do certain things.**

EXAMPLE: What are we going to need?
Are we going to have music and games?
I'll bring the paper cups and paper plates.
I'll teach everyone games from my country.
I'll fix dessert.

---

*F. **Beyond the book: What's one of your favorite foods from your country that you might prepare for the potluck party? How will you prepare it? Use *will* and *be going to* when you write the recipe (directions) for it. Then exchange recipes with a partner.**

EXAMPLE: Name of Dish: Tzatziki
Type of Dish: Appetizer (Greek dip for bread)

1. First, I'm going to mix 4 cups of yogurt with 1 cup of sour cream.
2. Next, I'll peel a medium cucumber, remove the seeds, and chop it.
3. Then I'm going to mince 3 or 4 cloves of garlic.
4. I'll mix all of this together and add a little lemon juice, dill, and maybe some mint.

These verbs may help you:
bake = cook in the oven
saute = fry in butter
chop = cut into small pieces
whip = beat quickly
stir = mix slowly with a spoon

roast = cook meat or vegetables
  in the oven
mince = chop into very small pieces
boil = cook in very hot water
fry = cook in a frying pan

PART TWO / The Future Continuous Tense

● Reading Menus

The Future Continuous Tense: Statements

Subject	*will* (*not*)	*be*	Verb-*ing*
He	will[1]	be	starting a new job.
They	won't	be	opening early tomorrow.

Questions

Question Word	*will* (*not*)	*be*	Verb-*ing*
What	will	be	happening?
Who	won't	be	coming?

Question Word	*will* (*not*)	Subject	*be*	Verb-*ing*
Why	won't	he	be	fixing dessert?
What time	will	they	be	opening?

You can use the future continuous tense for an action that will be in progress at a definite time in the future.

> I'll be starting my new job <u>tomorrow</u>.
> They'll be serving lunch <u>at 1:00</u>. (= before 1:00, at 1:00, and probably after 1:00)

You can also use the future continuous tense to emphasize the (long) duration of a future action or for a repeated future action.

> She'll be working at the cash register <u>all day</u>.
> They'll by running back and forth to the kitchen <u>a lot</u>. (= very often)

Don't use the future continuous tense with nonaction verbs. Instead, use the simple future tense. For lists of nonaction verbs, see pages 28 and 30.

[1] Contractions are common with pronouns:
I'll, you'll, it'll, he'll, she'll, we'll, they'll.

A.

Freddy is going to begin his new job tomorrow. What will be happening in the restaurant at 12:30? Make questions and answers with the cue words. Use the future continuous tense. Follow the example.

EXAMPLE: 1. a. What will Freddy be doing (at 12:30 tomorrow)?
  b. He'll be clearing a table.

1. a. (What / Freddy) do
   b. (He) clear a table

2. a. (Why / he) hurry *why will he be hurrying*
   b. (People) wait for tables *because they will be waiting for tables*

3. a. (What / the hostess) do *what will the hostess be doing*
   b. (She) try to find an empty table *she will be trying to find an empty table*

4. a. (Where / a policeman) sit
   b. (He) sit at the counter

Homework

5. a. (Who / he) talk to
   b. (He) talk to a waitress

6. a. (What / one customer) do
   b. (He) try to catch the waitress's eye

7. a. (How / people) eat fried chicken
   b. (They) eat it with their fingers

8. a. (Where / people) pay their bills
   b. (They) take them to the cash register

B.

Discuss or write about your plans for this evening, tomorrow morning, and tomorrow at lunch time. What time will you be having dinner? What will you be having for breakfast? Where will you be having lunch tomorrow?

EXAMPLES: I'll be having dinner tonight at 6:30.
  I'll be eating some cereal for breakfast tomorrow.

C.   Mac's Family Restaurant, where Freddy begins work tomorrow, is going to have a new menu next week. How will this change things at the restaurant? Use the future continuous tense to answer the questions and tell what will be happening when the restaurant starts to use the new menu. Make complete sentences.

MAC'S FAMILY RESTAURANT open 7:00 a.m. - 11:00 p.m.

BREAKFAST (served all day)

1. two eggs, any style, ham, toast, & jam	$3.00
2. french toast, fruit cup	$2.75
3. stack of four buttermilk pancakes, maple syrup	$1.95
4. steak and eggs, hashed brown potatoes	$5.75

Side Orders

fresh fruit (in season)	$1.50
toast (white or wheat)	.75
hashed brown potatoes	.95

Beverages

coffee, tea	.75
fruit juice	$1.00
milk	.85

LUNCH

Sandwiches

Hamburger Deluxe—1/3 lb. beef, lettuce, tomatoes	$3.75
Tuna Delight	$3.50
Club Sandwich—turkey, bacon, lettuce, tomato on white toast	$4.25

Salads

Seafood Salad shrimp & crab on lettuce	$5.50
Pasta Salad pasta, olives, tomatoes	$3.95
Dieter's Delight assorted fresh vegetables, hard-boiled egg, chicken	$4.75

Children's Plate (for kids under 12) hamburger, french fries, small salad, milk or cola ... $2.50

DINNER

Chicken, roasted or fried, rice or noodles, dinner salad	$6.75
Vegetarian Platter—an assortment of fresh vegetables and fruits	$6.00
Baked Halibut—fresh, boneless fish with vegetables & your choice of rice or potatoes	$6.75
Chef's Special Salad	$5.00
Roast Beef with vegetables and baked potato	$5.25

Desserts

ice cream	$1.50
fresh fruit (in season)	$2.00
chocolate cake	$1.75
carrot cake	$1.75
fresh fruit pie (apple, peach)	$1.75
a la mode	.50

Early-Bird Specials—
$1.00 off all entrees—4:00-5:30 p.m.
10% discount for seniors

---

1. What time will the restaurant be opening? *The restaurant will be opening at 7:00.*

2. Who will be getting a discount? *The seniors will be getting a discount*

3. When will people be having breakfast? *the people will be having breafast all day*

4. What will the restaurant owners be serving with french toast? *the restaurant owners will be serving fruit cup w. the french toast*

5. When will they be offering fresh fruit? *they be offering fresh fruit in season.*

6. How much will they be charging for a cup of coffee? *they be chargeing .75 for a cup of coffee?*

7. What kinds of sandwiches will they be serving? *they be serving Hamburger*

8. What time will people be coming for dinner if they want to save money? *they will be coming between 4:00 to 5:30 PM.*

PART THREE / The Conditional (Future Possible)

● Avoiding Food Poisoning

The Conditional

A sentence in the conditional has two parts: the cause or the condition and the result. There are two possible ways to place these parts.

> If he <u>isn't</u> sure the potato salad is safe to eat, he'll <u>throw</u> it out.
>   (cause   (result)
> or condition)

> He'll <u>throw</u> the potato salad out if he <u>isn't</u> sure it is safe to eat.
> (result)   (cause
>   or condition)

The verb after *if* in the cause or condition is in the simple present tense (or sometimes in the present continuous tense), but the meaning is future. The verb in the result is future.

Instead of a result, sometimes the sentence expresses advice or possibility. Use *should* or *ought to* for <u>advice</u> and use *may, might,* or *could* for <u>possibility</u> + the simple form of the verb. The meaning is present or future.

> If you <u>aren't</u> sure the chicken is good, you <u>should</u> throw it out.

Alquilar

A. **At the restaurant, Mac hired two new cooks at the same time he hired Freddy. These cooks are each trying to avoid the jobs they don't like. What do they suggest to each other? Make affirmative sentences with the words from the lists below the picture. Use the conditional.**

EXAMPLE: Ivan: I'll wash the lettuce if you chop the onions.

Ivan doesn't want to:

chop the onions
take out the garbage
fry the chicken
Picar mince the garlic
write out the shopping list
clean the spinach

Charles doesn't want to:

wash the lettuce
clean out the refrigerators
slice the bread
crema whip the egg whites
organize the shelves
bake the pies

till death do us part
till debt do us part

love at first sight
love at purse sight

B. To avoid arguments, Ivan and Charles each agree not to do certain things. What do they promise each other? Make negative sentences with the words from the lists below.

EXAMPLE: Ivan won't yell at Charles if Charles doesn't yell at Ivan.

Ivan promises not to:

yell at Charles
tell Charles what to do
forget to clean the stove
turn off the radio while they work
avoid the hard jobs
take a coffee break at busy times

Charles promises not to:

yell at Ivan
forget to do his own job
forget to take out the garbage
turn up the volume so high
avoid the hard jobs
leave the kitchen to call his
   girlfriend every hour

C. Make sentences of advice with the cue words. Use the conditional. Follow the example.

EXAMPLE: **1. a.** What should you do if you have an opened jar of mayonnaise?
        b. If we have an opened jar of mayonnaise, we should keep it in the refrigerator.

 1. a. What should you do if you have an opened jar of mayonnaise?
     b. (we) keep it in the refrigerator

2. a. What should someone do if he finds an unopened can with a puffed top?
     b. (he) throw it away immediately to avoid poisoning from botulism

3. a. What should a cook do if he prepares chicken in a bowl?
     b. (he) wash the bowl and all utensils before he uses them again

4. a. What should you do if you use poultry or eggs in a recipe?
     b. (we) cook them completely to avoid salmonella poisoning

5. a. What should people do if they think they have food poisoning?
     b. (they) call a doctor immediately

6. a. What should a family do if they go on a picnic on a hot day?
     b. (they) not eat warm dairy or poultry products

PART FOUR / Two-Word Verbs: Inseparable and Separable

Inseparable Two-Word Verbs

Some two-word verbs are inseparable; that is, a direct object can't come between the verb and the preposition.

> Did she call on you?
>
> Did she call ~~you on~~?

Some of these two-word verbs and their meanings are below. The verbs marked with a star (*) do not take an object.

break up* = separate (as in divorce)
call on = visit (formal), or ask someone to answer or speak
catch up* = reach the same place as another person
come along* = accompany, come with
come over* = come to someone's home or office
dress up* = put on special clothes
drop in* = drop by = visit informally, without an invitation
get over = recover from (a sickness or a bad situation), get well
give up = quit, stop trying, lose hope

hear from = receive a letter or phone call from
keep on = continue
look for = try to find
look into = investigate, try to find an answer
make up* = end an argument, apologize
run into = meet a person by chance, or crash into
run away* = try to escape, or leave home without telling parents
show up* = appear, arrive
take after = look like or be like (parents or grandparents)
take off* = leave (usually by plane)

Separable Two-Word Verbs

Other two-word verbs are separable; that is, a direct object can come between the verb and the preposition.

> They called | Francisco up.
> | him up.

If the object is a noun, it can come after the preposition.

> They called up Francisco.

If the object is a pronoun, it cannot come after the preposition.

> They called up ~~him~~.

Some of these two-word verbs and their meanings are below.

bring back = return
call up = telephone
check off = mark an item on a list
clean out (a closet, etc.) = take everything out, throw or give some things away, and put the rest of the things back in order
clean up[1] = make neat and in order
cross out = remove (a word, etc.) by drawing a line through
do over = do again
figure out = solve
fill out = write information in the blank spaces on an application form
give back = return
hand in = give (a report, exam, etc.) to a teacher or employer
look up = look for information in a dictionary or other reference book
pick out = choose
put away = put something in its proper place

put off = postpone, do something at a later time
show off = show something proudly
take back = return
take off = remove (clothing, jewelry, etc.)
take out = remove the garbage, or escort a person to dinner, a movie, etc.
tear down = destroy (a building, etc.)
tear up = destroy (a street, piece of paper)
think over = think about, consider
throw away = discard, put in a trash can
throw out = throw away
try on = try or test (clothing) for fit or appearance
turn down = decrease volume; or say "no" to a job or other offer
turn off = shut off (T.V., stereo, lights, etc.)
turn on = start or put on (T.V., stereo, lights. etc.)
turn up[2] = increase volume; or appear, arrive
use up = use all of something

[1]This verb usually has no object when it means "everything."

[2]This verb has no object in the second meaning.

A. What happened the day after the party? Study the lists of two-word verbs on page 71. Then choose the correct two-word verb from the list below for each blank in the exercise. You may use some more than once. Be sure to choose the correct position for each object, if there is one.

EXAMPLES:
1. The day after the party, the students tore down the decorations
2. and threw them away.

call up	figure out	look for	show up	√ throw away
clean up	get over	pick out	take back	turn on
come over	give up	put away	√ tear down	

The day after the party, the students ___*tear down*___ and ___*throw*___

                                    1. destroyed the decorations   **2.** put them

___*away*___. Many people ___*come over*___ to help ___*clean up*___.

in the trash   **3.** came to the house   **4.** make everything neat and in order

Francisco was trying to ___*get over*___, so he wasn't really able to help much,

              5. recover from a terrible headache

but he ___*put away*___ and helped the others ___*look for*___

       6. put the clean dishes in their proper place   **7.** try to find a lost ring

_____. They _____ for half an hour, but it never ___*show up*___.

          8. tried to find it   **9.** appeared

They couldn't ___*figure out*___.

     10. solve it

Francisco was planning to ___*take back*___, but his headache soon got

            11. return the borrowed chairs

worse, so he ___*give up*___ and went home. Junichiro ___*come over*___.

     12. stopped trying   **13.** returned them

Even though they were working, it was a pleasant afternoon. Minh ___*pick out*___

                            14. chose some records

_____ and ___*turn on*___. And several people ___*call up*___ to

     15. started the stereo   **16.** telephoned them

thank them for the party.

CHAPTER 5

Getting Along

GRAMMAR:
The present perfect tense with *since* and *for* and with certain verbs to express continuation
The present perfect continuous tense
Tag questions
Article usage: nonspecific and specific nouns

COMPETENCIES:
Obtaining information about helplines and hotlines
Understanding types of counseling services
Returning things to a store
Getting help with consumer problems
Obtaining information about transportation for the handicapped and elderly and about legal assistance

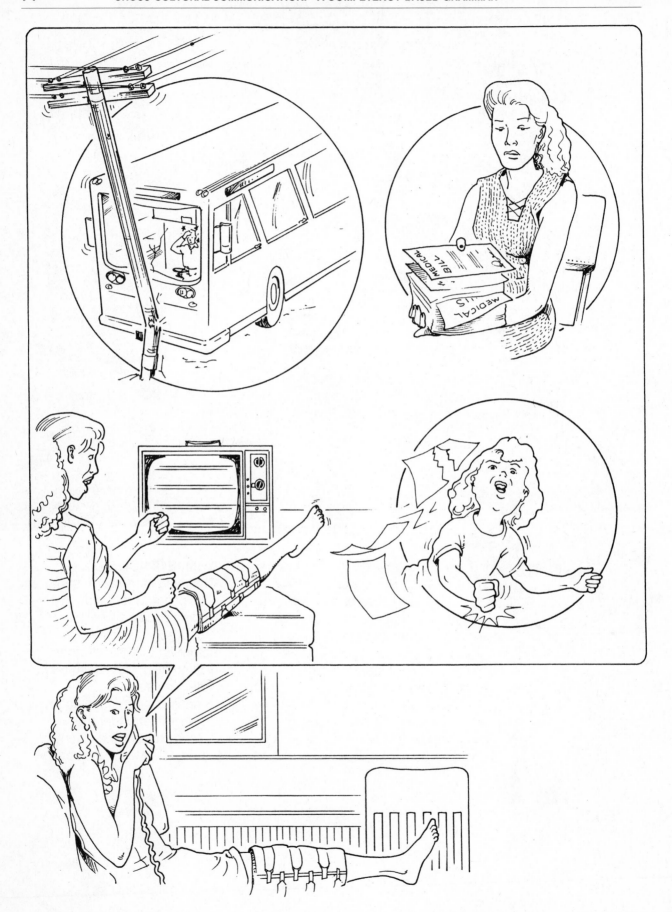

How much do you already know? Read the following paragraphs and circle the correct answers.

"Hi, Jean. This is Betty. I haven't seen you for such a long time. How have you been?"

"Well, I don't know what [was/has been] wrong with me [for/since] the past few months.
1.   2.
You don't know a good, inexpensive doctor, [do you/don't you]? I [didn't sleep/haven't been
3.   4.
sleeping] well ever [for/since] my daughter and I [were/have been] in [an/the] accident two
5.   6.   7.
months ago. My leg has been in [a/the] brace nine hours every day since [an/the] accident, and I
8.   9.
can't go to work or classes because I can't climb the steps of the bus with [a/the] brace on. You
10.
can't suggest a way for me to get help with transportation, [can you/you can]? Also, I don't have
11.
money to pay all these medical bills. I need to sue [a/the] bus company that caused the accident,
12.
but I don't know how to find a lawyer. Say, you used to have a good lawyer, [haven't you/didn't
13.
you]?"

"It's really terrible to be home alone all day, especially when my television hasn't been working
well [for/since] several weeks. I [have tried/have been trying] four times to get the store to give
14.   15.
me a refund or a new T.V., but with no luck. You wouldn't know who I could call for help with this
problem, [could I/would you]?"
16.

"Of course, I have [gotten/been] especially anxious about my daughter ever since I [realized/
17.   18.
have realized] that she [had/has been having] serious emotional problems for quite a long time,
19.
and I don't know how to find a psychologist to help her."

"Well, it's certainly been nice to have this little visit, [isn't it/hasn't it]?"
20.

score: _____

20

PART ONE
The Present Perfect Tense with *since* and *for* and with Certain Verbs to Express Continuation

● Obtaining Information about Helplines and and Hotlines

The Present Perfect Tense with *since* and *for*

Subject	*have* (*not*)	Past Participle
I	have	known this for a while.
You	have	been anxious all morning.
Jean	hasn't	felt well since then.
We	have always	shared our feelings.
They	haven't	wanted or needed help.[1]

The past participles of regular verbs are the same as the past tense (*-ed*). Many irregular past participles are also the same as the past tense (such as *find—found—found* and *buy—bought—bought*). Some past participles are completely different from the past tense (such as *drive—drove—driven* and *shrink—shrank—shrunk*). Lists of irregular past participles are in the appendixes, page 179-180. Use contractions whenever possible with the present perfect: *I've, you've, she's, he's, it's, we've, they've.*

You can use the present perfect tense for an activity that is happening now. However, it is different from the two present tenses because something in the sentence or context tells when the action began or how long it has happened.

You often use the present perfect tense with the words *since* and *for*. The verb in a clause after *since* will be in the simple past tense: My life has changed *since* the accident *occurred.*

since	*for*
9:30	five hours
yesterday	one day
last week	the past week
last year	the last year
December	a year
June 12	several weeks
the accident	a long time
he got up	two hours

You can also use the present perfect with words and expressions such as *always, so far, all morning* (*afternoon, day,* etc.), and *in the past week* (*month, few hours,* etc.).

[1] When there are two present perfect verbs, don't repeat *have* if you don't repeat the subject.

A. **Complete the sentences below with the present perfect tense of each verb in parentheses. Then circle _for_ or _since_.**

EXAMPLES: **1. a.** How long have you worked here at Helpline?

　　　　　b. I've worked here for three years.

1. a. How long ___have___ you ___worked___ (work) here at Helpline?

b. I ___'ve worked___ (work) here [for / since] three years.

2. a. What ___have___ the main purpose of Helpline ___being___ (be)?

b. Well, we'___re not tryed___ (not try) to offer direct help [for / since] the past

year. Instead, our purpose [for / since] last December ___was___ (be) to answer

people's questions about where to find help.

3. a. How many calls ___have___ Helpline ___took___ (take) [for / since] you opened?

b. Oh, it's hard to say. We'___re not kept___ (not keep) an exact record. Each worker

here ___answered___ (answer) thirty to forty calls every day [for / since] the

last few years.

4. **a.** What kinds of problems _have_ you _helped_ (help) people with?

   b. Oh, we _'ve told_ (tell) elderly and handicapped people where to find

   transportation. We _'ve sent_ (send) many people to a legal aid service

   for free advice from a lawyer. And each of us _'ve helped_ (help) people

   find inexpensive counseling for emotional problems. We _'ve attempt_ (not

   attempt) to give psychological help [for / <u>since</u>] last year. Instead, we _'ve transfered_

   (transfer) our callers to other crisis centers [<u>for</u> / since] the past twelve months.

The Present Perfect Tense with Certain Verbs to Express Continuation

You can use the present perfect tense with certain verbs to express the
continuation of an activity that began in the past, but use the simple past tense
to express the beginning of an action.

> They've been married for ten years. (They are still married. The
> marriage is not finished.)
>
> They got married ten years ago. (The marriage ceremony is finished.
> They began to be married ten years ago.)

Some of these verbs are:

Beginning	Continuation
catch (a cold, etc.) ⟶	have (a cold, etc.)
find out/realize ⟶	know/understand
get/become ⟶	be
get/receive/buy ⟶	have/own
go to bed ⟶	sleep
join (a club) ⟶	belong to (a club)
learn ⟶	know
meet ⟶	know
pick up ⟶	hold
put on ⟶	wear

B. **Make questions and answers about the chart. Use the present perfect and simple past tenses. Follow the examples. (Pretend that today is Friday.)**

EXAMPLES: 1. a. How long has Jean known about Dial-A-Ride?

b. She's known about it since Monday (for four days).

a. How did she find out about Dial-A-Ride?

b. She found out about it from Helpline.

How long?

	Sat.	Sun.	Mon.	Tues.	Wed.	Thurs.	Today
1. how?			find out about Dial-A-Ride (from Helpline)	. . . .			know about Dial-A-Ride
2. why?				buy a new T.V. (because her old one didn't work)	. . . .		have a new T.V.
3. why?					join (because she couldn't afford a private psychologist)	. . . .	belong to a self-help counseling group
4. where?						learn about the legal aid service (through the white pages of the phone book)	know about a legal aid service
5. what?	make her depressed (her problems)	. . . .					be depressed
6. why?			put on a new brace (because the old one didn't fit)	. . . .			wear a new brace
7. when?				realize that consumers are not powerless (when she talked with Jim at Helpline)	. . . .		know how to handle a consumer problem

C.

Make questions and answers with the cue words. Use the present perfect and simple past tenses. Use *for* or *since* in the answers. Follow the examples.

EXAMPLE:
1. **a.** Have you worked at Helpline for a long time?
   b. I've worked here since last June. Before that, I worked on a crisis hotline.

1. **a.** ~~have~~ (you) work at Helpline
   b. last June *I've worked here*
      work on a crisis hotline

 HELPLINE

2. **a.** ~~have~~ (you) need~~ed~~ a day-care center for your child
   b. the past month *I've need a daycar* ~~since~~ *post month*
      before that I take her to a babysitter

 CHILD-CARE HELPLINE

3. **a.** ~~have~~ (your husband) beat you *He've beat you since he lost his job and started drinking*
   b. he lost his job and started drinking
      before that he was be never violent

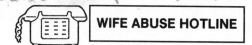 WIFE ABUSE HOTLINE

4. **a.** ~~has~~ (your daughter) feel anxious *for long time?*
   b. we were in an accident *She has feel anxious since we were in a accident*
      before, that, she was be fine

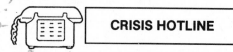 CRISIS HOTLINE

5. **a.** ~~has~~ (your landlord) refuse to repair things *for long time? since the post month*
   b. the past month *He've refuse to repair things since post month*
      before that complain about it, but he fix things *I didn't* *fixed*

 RENTERS' ACTION HOTLINE

6. **a.** *How long* ~~has~~ (this man) sleep on the streets
   b. several months *He've sleep on the streets for several months*
      before that, he had have a good job and an apartment

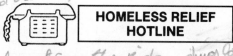 HOMELESS RELIEF HOTLINE

7. **a.** *How long* ~~has~~ (your son) be on drugs *He has been drugs since he met some other kids on drugs last month*
   b. he met some other kids on drugs last month
      before that he never take any drugs *was*

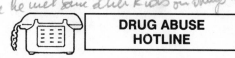 DRUG ABUSE HOTLINE

*D.

Beyond the book: Go to the white pages of the phone book. How many community services can you find that have hotlines or information helplines? What kind of services are these? Discuss these with other students. Did you have helplines or hotlines in your country? Have you known about helplines and hotlines for a long time, or did you learn about them in this chapter?

PART TWO / The Present Perfect Continuous Tense

● Understanding Types of Counseling Services

The Present Perfect Continuous Tense

Subject	*have (not)*	*been*	Verb-*ing*
I	have[1]	been	having problems with my teenager.
This group	has	been	meeting together for two months.
They	haven't	been	taking drugs or drinking[2] since they began this program.

You can use the present perfect continuous tense for an action that is happening now if you express a time frame (how long it has been going on) or if you are emphasizing the continuation of the action.

> She's been coming here for the past few months.
> They've been sitting there since 9:30.
> I don't know how long he has been waiting.

You can use this tense with expressions such as *since, for, all day,* and *in the past week.* Other such expressions are listed on page 76. Sometimes the time expression is not in the sentence. It is only in the mind of the speaker or writer.

[1] As with the present perfect tense, use contractions whenever possible.

[2] As with other tenses, don't repeat the auxiliary verbs if you don't repeat the subject.

PEER COUNSELING GROUP

A. **Make questions and answers with the words below. Follow the example. Use the present perfect continuous tense and be sure that your answer is logical.**

EXAMPLE: **a.** How has your son been dealing with the death of his father?

b. He's been dealing with it better than I expected.

Questions

| How long
Why
How | you
your son
your daughter
your husband
your wife | have trouble sleeping
think about suicide
look for a job
deal with the death of his father
take drugs
suffer from cancer
suffer from depression
consider a divorce
handle your son's alcoholism
deal with this fear | ? |

suffer = sufrir

Answers

I He She	for since	the accident over a year last month the past few months a long time last year the boss fired me/him/her
	because	we've had such problems I've been so worried
	not very well better than I expected	

The Present Perfect Continuous vs. the Present Perfect

Don't use the present perfect continuous tense with:

1. frequency adverbs such as *never*, *often*, and *always*;
2. a specific amount or a specific number of times such as *$53.00, twice, several times*, or *27 pounds*; or
3. nonaction verbs (see pages 28 and 30).

Instead, use the present perfect tense in these cases.

B. In the following conversation, fill in the blanks with the correct tense: the present perfect continuous or, if that's not possible, the present perfect.

EXAMPLE: **1.** How long have you been having problems with your marriage?

Counselor: How long ___*had*___ you ___*been*___ problems with your marriage?
1. have

Wife: Well, I think that I ___*know*___ almost since the beginning that we ___*not*___
2. know   **3.** not

___*communicating*___ well.
communicate

Husband: So have I. But I ___*don't want*___ to admit it.
4. not want

Counselor: What do you mean when you say "not communicating"? ___*been*___ there _____
5. be

a language problem?

Husband: Oh, no. Although my wife is Xenrovian, and I'm from Canada, we ___*never had*___
6. never have

___*been having*___ trouble with language. We speak each other's languages fluently.

Counselor: Well, can you each give me an example of something that ___*bothering*___
7. bother

you that you ___*never communicated*___ to the other?
8. never communicate

Wife: Yes. He doesn't ever notice if I lose weight or have a new hairstyle. For example, I

___*had been losing*___ a lot of weight in the past month. I ___*lose*___ almost fifteen
9. lose   **10.** lose

pounds, but he ___*has mention*___ it even once. This ___*has been*___
11. not mention   **12.** irritate

___*irritating*___ me a lot.

Husband: (*surprised*) But you _____ so!
13. never say

Wife: I wanted to be polite. I didn't want to start an argument.

Counselor: (*turning to the husband*) All right. And you?

Husband: Well, I know that I _____ my books, papers, clothes, and
14. not keep

sports stuff in order for the past few months because I _____ busy.
15. be

But it _____ me crazy when she rearranges my things. I
16. always drive

_____ it when she moves my stuff around.
17. always hate

Wife: (*surprised*) But I didn't know! You _____ a single word about this.
18. not say

Husband: I didn't want to hurt your feelings.

Counselor: Aha! Now I see. It seems that you two _____ too hard to be
19. try

polite. You _____ open and honest with each other. You both
20. not be

_____ your true feelings. This _____
21. hide   22. cause

your problems.

_____ **C.** **Correct the underlined mistakes in the following paragraphs.**

EXAMPLE: 1. Jean has been bringing her daughter to see a counselor at the Glenview Mental Health Clinic
              2. for the past week.

Jean <u>has been brought</u> her daughter to see a counselor at the Glenview Mental Health Clinic
     1.

<u>since the past week</u>. The child <u>was</u> depressed ever since her parents <u>have gotten</u> a divorce last year,
2.   3.   4.

and she <u>has been had</u> nightmares since she and her mother <u>have been</u> in an accident. Jean <u>has been</u>
      5.   6.   7.

<u>needing</u> to be very careful with money <u>since quite a long time</u>, so when she <u>has realized</u> that her
                                     8.   9.

daughter needed psychological help, she <u>didn't thought</u> that she could afford it. But then one day
                                               10.

her friend Betty <u>has told</u> her about an information service called Helpline. From Helpline she <u>has</u>
                 11.   12.

<u>found out</u> about this clinic, where people pay on a "sliding scale"; that is, they pay only what they

can afford, or they go to a free peer counseling group. Jean and her daughter <u>have been coming</u>
                                                               13.

here two times in the past week, and Jean <u>have been felt</u> hopeful that her daughter will come out of
                                       14.

her depression soon.

Eric <u>been</u> a member of the Ex-Drug-Abusers Support Group <u>since he has given up</u> drugs four
      15.   16.

months ago. The group <u>helped</u> him a lot <u>since these past few months</u>. Although it <u>not been</u> easy, he
                   17.   18.   19.

<u>has never been taking</u> drugs since he <u>has been joining</u> the group. He <u>has been learn</u> that life is
20.   21.   22.

more enjoyable without drugs. The group <u>has also teaching</u> him that other people are "in the same
                                           23.

boat." He is not alone; other people are in the same situation.

_____ ***D.** **Beyond the book: Tell or write about someone you know who has been having problems. Don't give the person's name, but explain what kind of problem this person has and how he or she has been dealing with it.**

PART THREE / Tag Questions

● Returning Things to a Store ● Getting Help with Consumer Problems

Tag Questions

You can make a statement into a question if you add a "tag." For affirmative statements, the tag is negative. For negative statements, the tag is affirmative. The subject in a tag is always a pronoun. If the statement contains *be* or an auxiliary verb, use it in the tag.

> She's a consumer protection expert, <u>isn't she</u>?
> You'll be here, <u>won't you</u>?
> They've been arguing a lot, <u>haven't they</u>?
> The psychologist can help, <u>can't she</u>?
> I should talk more openly with him, <u>shouldn't I</u>?

> That T.V. isn't working, <u>is it</u>?
> The salesperson won't give you a refund, <u>will he</u>?
> You haven't told him, <u>have you</u>?
> He didn't want to go to a counselor, <u>did he</u>?
> Those people couldn't accept it, <u>could they</u>?

If there is no auxiliary verb in the statement, use a form of the verb *do* in the tag.

> You have the number of the Better Business Bureau, <u>don't you</u>?
> They called Helpline, <u>didn't they</u>?

If you use "I am" as the subject and verb in the statement, use the verb *aren't* in the tag in conversational English.

> I'm in trouble, <u>aren't I</u>?

A.   **Add a tag to complete each question below.**

EXAMPLE: **1.** You've done something to this fine T.V., haven't you?

   1. You've done something to this fine T.V., _____?

   2. It was working well until you took it home, _____?

   3. You didn't remember to adjust the color, _____?

   4. You know about the antenna, _____?

   5. Your children haven't been playing with it, _____?

   6. I can't possibly refund your money without an okay from my boss, _____?

   7. You don't have your receipt, _____?

   8. You wouldn't want to come back later, _____?

CALL FOR ACTION

   9. You saved your receipt, _____?

   10. You've taken the T.V. and your receipt back to the store, _____?

   11. They realize that you have a warranty, _____?

   12. You don't care if they refund your money or exchange the T.V. for another one, _____?

   13. The department manager wasn't there when you were at the store, _____?

   14. It doesn't seem like this store wants to have repeat customers, _____?

   15. You'd like me to call the store for you, _____?

   16. You'll be home later if I need to call you back, _____?

B. **Make questions and answers with the cue words. Use tag questions. Follow the examples.**

EXAMPLES:
1. **a.** I need the receipt, don't I?
   b. Yes, I guess you do.
   a. I thought so.

2. **a.** The company doesn't offer a warranty, does it?
   b. No, I guess it doesn't.
   a. I didn't think so.

1. **a.** (I) need the receipt
   b. yes

2. **a.** (the company) doesn't offer a warranty
   b. no

3. **a.** (I) should talk to the manager
   b. yes

4. **a.** (you) kept a copy of your letter to the store
   b. yes

5. **a.** (they) are suggesting that you write the manufacturer
   b. yes

6. **a.** (you) haven't written to the Better Business Bureau
   b. no

7. **a.** (I) don't have to have a lawyer in small claims court
   b. no

8. **a.** (the store) doesn't have any more of these pillows on sale
   b. no

9. **a.** (you) can give me a "raincheck" so that I can get one later at the same price
   b. yes

10. **a.** (Call for Action) helps people with many different consumer problems
    b. yes

11. **a.** (I) can probably find Call for Action on a radio station in this city
    b. yes

*C. **Beyond the book: With a partner or in a small group, discuss consumer problems and their solutions. Use as many tag questions as possible in your discussion.**

EXAMPLES: You've sometimes needed to return something to a store, haven't you? What do you usually do when this happens?

You didn't know about Call for Action before this lesson, did you? How do you usually deal with consumer problems?

PART FOUR / Article Usage: Nonspecific and Specific Nouns

● Obtaining Information about Transportation for the Handicapped and Elderly and about Legal Assistance

---

Articles with Nonspecific Nouns

To speak in general of everything or anything in a certain group, you can use (1) *a* or *an* + a singular count noun or (2) no article (∅) + a plural count noun. You can also use (3) no article (∅) + a noncount noun.

> A marriage counselor is a person who helps people with marriage problems.
>> Which marriage counselor? Any one in the world.
>> Which people? Any people.
>> Which marriage problems? Any marriage problems.

> Love is important in marriage.
>> Which love? Love in general.
>> Which marriage? Marriage in general.

You can also use (1) *a* or *an* + a singular count noun, (2) no article (∅) + a plural count noun, or (3) no article (∅) + a noncount noun the first time you mention something.

> He rented an apartment that had nice furniture and big closets.

Articles with Specific Nouns

Use *the* for the second (third, fourth, etc.) time you mention something.

> The apartment was sunny, and he liked the furniture and appreciated the closets.

Use *the* (even at the first mention) if it is clear which one you are talking about.

> Although he liked the apartment, he soon found that the landlord often tried to avoid fixing things such as the plumbing.
>> Which apartment? The apartment he rented.
>> Which landlord? The landlord of the apartment building.
>> Which plumbing? The plumbing in the apartment.

A. For each blank, choose a, an, the, or Ø (no article).

EXAMPLE: 1. On Monday morning, a blue van from Dial-A-Ride came to pick Jean up.

On Monday morning, _____ blue van from Dial-A-Ride came to pick Jean up. _____ van
.................................1. ....2.

stopped several times to pick up elderly people and people with _____ handicaps. _____ people
....3. ....4.

who rode _____ van made _____ appointments each week for the next week. _____ van had
.............5. ....6. ....7.

_____ special device to help them up _____ steps.
8. ....9.

This day, Jean was on her way to meet _____ lawyer from a legal aid organization. She had
....10.

learned from _____ person at Helpline that legal aid was _____ service for _____ people who
......................11. ....12. ....13.

needed _____ legal advice but couldn't pay _____ lawyer because they didn't make much money
...........14. ....15.

or didn't have _____ job. _____ person at Helpline also told her about _____ service called
.....................16. ....17. ....18.

Lawyer Referral Service, which is _____ group of lawyers who help _____ clients who can pay
....19. ....20.

some amount, but not much.

Anyway, when she got to the legal aid office and talked with _____ lawyer, Jean found out
....21.

that many lawyers would help her with her lawsuit on a contingency basis; that is, they would

charge her _____ fee if they won _____ lawsuit but not if they lost.
.................22. ....23.

Jean decided to sue _____ bus company that was responsible for _____ accident in which
.........................24. ....25.

she hurt her leg. She needed _____ help to pay _____ medical bills from that accident.
...............................26. ....27.

*B. Beyond the book: In a small group, discuss transportation in your community. How do you get to school each day? As you tell your group about your route to school, be sure to use articles correctly.

EXAMPLE: I get on a bus at the corner of 5th and Oak. The bus is always crowded with people who are going to work. I get off the bus after about a mile. Then I walk past a post office and a bookstore. Sometimes I stop at the post office to mail a letter. I cross the street and go through the front gate of the school.

Discuss the transportation problems of elderly and handicapped people. How might you find a service such as Dial-A-Ride (perhaps with a different name) in your community? Do you know anyone who needs such a service?

*C. Beyond the book: With a partner or in a small group, discuss legal problems that you or your friends have had. How did you solve them? Check a phone book for legal aid services in your city. What services are available?

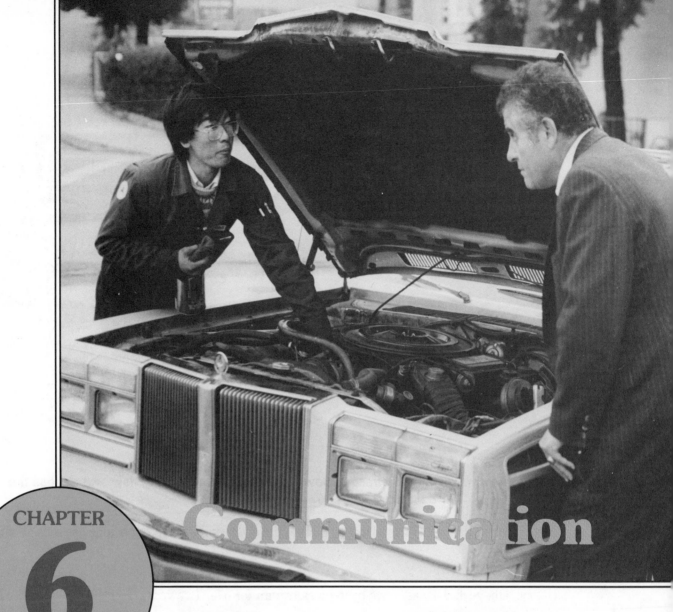

CHAPTER 6

Communication

GRAMMAR:
The present perfect vs.
the simple past tense (I)
The present perfect vs.
the simple past tense (II)
The present perfect and the
simple past tenses: review
Prepositions of place

COMPETENCIES:
Describing car maintenance
Buying a car
Describing problems with
cars
Telling where places are

***How much do you already know*? Read the following interview and choose the correct words. Circle your answers.**

Ernie: Well, tell me, Harry, [did you have/have you had] much experience as a used-car
                          1.

salesman?

Harry: Oh, yeah. I [was/have been] a salesman for over five years. I [sold/have sold] cars
                2.   3.

for three years at a dealership [at/on] Main Street. After that, I [worked/have
                                4.   5.

worked] at that car lot (*he points*) [in front of/across the street from] here.
                                        6.

Ernie: Do you enjoy this line of work?

Harry: Oh, yeah. In my whole life, I [never want/have never wanted] to do anything
                                  7.

except be a salesman. I can sell anything to anyone—even if they don't want it.

Ernie: I see. How do you accomplish this?

Harry: Well, I [went/have gone] to dozens of sales meetings last year, and there [were/
            8.   9.

have been] at least ten more this year. I [learned/have learned] a lot about psychology
                                    10.

in my career as a salesman. This education [taught/has taught] me to make each
                                        11.

customer trust me. Of course, I [always knew/have always known] that it's important
                                    12.

to be friendly and polite...

Ernie: …and honest?

Harry: (*shrugs*) Well, as you know, honesty doesn't sell many cars. I [sold/have sold]
13.
hundreds of cars last year, and I [sold/have sold] twenty-three so far this year. My
14.
success [wasn't ever/hasn't ever been] due to total honesty. I tell the customers
15.
what they want to hear—except, of course, for the price. They trust me.

Ernie: (*nods*) Uh-huh. I see. Well, Harry, I think that's all. Do you have any questions for

me?

Harry: Just one. When are you going to decide on a person for this job?

Ernie: I [have still decided/have already decided]. You have the job. You start on
16.
Monday. Have you met our office manager?

Harry: No, I [haven't met her/haven't met her already]. Should I go to her office now?
17.

Ernie: No. I think she's at lunch. She'll be back [on/in] the office at 1:00. Until then, I
18.
want you to walk [on/around] the car lot and take a look at the cars and trucks
19.
that you'll be selling. Oh, and Harry, one thing: You must never be dishonest with

me.

Harry: (*smiles very widely*) Of course not. Trust me. I haven't lied to you [ever/yet], have I?
20.

score: _____
20

PART ONE / The Present Perfect vs. the Simple Past Tense (I)

● Describing Car Maintenance

Present Perfect	Simple Past
You can use the present perfect tense[1] for one action (or the repetition of an action) that is finished if the period of time in which it happened is not finished.	You can use the simple past tense for one action (or the repetition of an action) that is finished if the period of time in which it happened is also finished.
Ernie has interviewed several people this week.	Ernie didn't interview anyone last week.
Some expressions that are common with the present perfect tense are:	Some expressions that are common with the simple past tense are:
today this week (month, year) in the past five years in my life ever (= at any time in the life of a living person) never	yesterday last week (month, year) five years ago in his life (He's dead now.) ever (= at any time in the life of someone who is dead) never
Sometimes, the time expression is only in the mind of the speaker or writer—not in the sentence.	As with the present perfect tense, the time expression in the simple past tense is sometimes only in the mind of the speaker or writer.
Ernie has owned many used car lots. (in his life)	Ernie hired Harry. (yesterday)

[1] For the forms of the present perfect tense, see Chapter 5, page 76.

A. Use the cue words to make sentences about Ernie Lemon's great-grandfather (who died eighty years ago) and Ernie (who is still alive). Use the simple past tense and the present perfect tense. Follow the example.

EXAMPLE: 1. Ernie's great-grandfather was married only once.
            Ernie has been married three times.

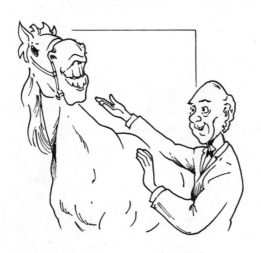 

1. be married only once   be married three times

2. work alone   hire dozens of employees

3. sell thousands of horses and carriages   sell thousands of cars and trucks

4. take a ship to Alaska once   never be to Alaska[1]

5. fight with customers a few times   not ever fight with customers

6. ride a horse every day   not ever ride a horse

7. drive an automobile once   drive hundreds of cars

8. not ever be arrested   be arrested twice

9. sometimes feel guilty about cheating   not ever feel guilty about cheating people
   people

[1] *Be to = go to* only with the present perfect or past perfect tenses.

_____ **B.** **Anita and Richard used to take good care of their car, so it ran well for several years. But they haven't taken very good care of it recently, so they've been having trouble with it. Make questions and answers with the cue words. Begin each question with *how often...* and use the simple past and present perfect tenses for the verbs. Follow the example.**

EXAMPLE: **1.** a: How often did they check the transmission fluid last year?
                   b: They checked it six times.
                   a: How often have they checked it this year?
                   b: They haven't checked it at all.

	Last Year	This Year
1. check the transmission fluid	6	0
2. wash the car	50	4
3. check the air pressure in the tires	12	2
4. change the water in the radiator	2	0
5. change the spark plugs	2	0
6. take the car for a tune-up	every 5,000 miles	0
7. change the oil	every 3,000 miles	1
8. change the oil filter	every 3,000 miles	0
9. rotate the tires	every 5,000 miles	0
10. let their car overheat	0	3
11. run out of gas	0	2
12. have a flat tire	0	1

C. **For each blank, choose the simple past tense or the present perfect tense.**

EXAMPLE: 1. Have you ever brought your car to this garage before?

Mechanic: _____ you _____ your car to this garage before?
          1. ever bring

Anita: Yes. I _____ it in four months ago. The automobile club _____ it here
          2. bring   **3. tow**

that day just as they _____ today. I _____ a dead battery that day, and
                    4. do   **5. have**

you _____ in a new one.
      6. put

Mechanic: Well, what seems to be the problem this time?

Richard: We _____ trouble with the radiator several times in the past few
          7. have

months. All of the water _____ out twice this month, and the car
                    8. leak

_____.
9. overheat

Mechanic: It's pretty clear that you have a leak in either the radiator or a hose. _____
                                                          10. not have

you _____ someone fix it the first time it _____?
                                  11. happen

Richard: No. We _____ a lot of money on this car last year, but we _____ a lot
          12. spend   **13. have**

of other bills to worry about this year.

Mechanic: Well, are there any other problems with the car that you _____ care of

                                         14. not take

in the past few months?

Anita: (*sighs*) Yes. It _____ us trouble starting in the morning.

                    15. give

Mechanic: When _____ your last tune-up?

            16. be

Anita: (*a little embarrassed*) About 10,000 miles ago. I know, I know. That's terrible. But

we _____ other problems with the car this year that seemed more serious.

        17. have

Last month we _____ an oil leak on the floor of the garage, and a month ago

             18. notice

we _____ to have trouble with the transmission. The brakes _____

      19. begin   **20.** start

to give us problems several months ago, and we _____ three flat tires this fall.

                                        21. have

Mechanic: (*shaking his head*) _____ trading this car in on a different car?

            22. you ever consider

*D.

Beyond the book: Do you have a car? If so, answer the following questions. If not, ask these questions of someone who has one. Be sure to use the simple past and present perfect tenses correctly.

1. What problems have you had with your car in the past few months?

2. How often have you done the following in the past year?

> changed the oil?
> changed the oil filter?
> had someone lubricate the car?
> checked the air pressure in the tires?
> rotated the tires?
> taken the car for a tune-up?

PART TWO / The Present Perfect vs. the Simple Past Tense (II)

● Buying a Car

The Present Perfect

You can use the present perfect tense for a past action when the period of time is not specific (not known or not important). Sometimes the time expression is only in the mind of the speaker or writer.

 I've seen the car. (= at some unspecified time in the past)

Note the word order of sentences with the following time expressions:

 before = "before now" in affirmative and negative statements and questions
     Have you seen this car <u>before</u>?
     I've never seen it <u>before</u>.

   yet = "before now" in questions when the speaker expects that the activity has happened; it is also used in negative statements
     Have you seen the car <u>yet</u>?
     I haven't seen it <u>yet</u>.

  still = "before now" in negative statements when the speaker thinks that the activity should have happened but hasn't
     I <u>still</u> haven't seen it.

 already = "before now" in affirmative statements and questions when the speaker thinks that the activity has happened earlier than expected
     I've <u>already</u> seen it. or I've seen it <u>already</u>.

The Simple Past

You can use the simple past tense for a past action when the period of time is specific or known. As with the present perfect, sometimes the time expression is only in the mind of the speaker or writer. (See Chapter 3 for more information about the simple past tense.)

A.

Anita and Richard have found a book called *How to Buy Your Next Car*, and they've used it to help them prepare to buy a used car. What preparations have they made? Arrange the words in the following questions and answers in the correct order.

EXAMPLE: 1. Well, have you decided on the kind of car you want yet?

1. Anita: _____

well, / you / yet / the kind of car you want / decided on / have / ?

Richard: _____   _____

no, / haven't / I / decided / yet / .

2. Anita: _____

learned / I / from this book / have / that it's important to know / exactly what car we want / .

Richard: _____

you / what else / that book / told / has / ?

3. Anita: _____

that we should read car magazines and consumer reports / found out / I / have / .

Richard: _____

but / already / I / done that / have / .

4. Anita: _____

well, / have / with garage mechanics about different models / talked / you / yet / ?

Richard: _____

already / of course / talked with them / have / I / .

5. Anita: _____

you / talked with owners of cars that you're interested in / yet / have / ?

_____

and / have / yet / checked the "blue book" / you / to find out how much our old car is worth as a trade-in / ?

Richard: _____

I / found out / already / of course / have / the value of our car / .

6. Anita: _____

but / washed our old car and / had someone steam-clean the engine / you / have / ?

Richard: _____

what? / no, / still / done that / haven't / I / .   never even / I / heard of that / before / have / .

_____ **B.**   **Make questions and answers with the cue words. Use the present perfect tense for the underlined verbs. Follow the example.**

EXAMPLE: **1. a:** Have you studied the chapter on negotiation?
         b: Yes. I've already read it twice.

1. a: you / <u>study</u> the chapter on negotiation
   b: yes / I / already <u>read</u> it twice

2. a: you / <u>choose</u> the car you'd like / already
   b: yes / we / <u>choose</u> the model we're interested in

3. a: you / <u>decide</u> to use your car as a trade-in
   b: no / we / still / not <u>make up</u> our minds

4. a: your friend / <u>help</u> you buy a car / before
   b: yes / he / <u>have a</u> lot of experience as a mechanic

5. a: you / <u>decide</u> to sign the contract / yet
   b: no / we / not <u>take</u> the car for a test drive / yet

6. a: you / not <u>sell</u> them the car / yet
   b: no / they / still not <u>finish</u> inspecting it

7. a: the "blue book" / <u>help</u> you
   b: yes / it / <u>tell</u> me the fair price for this car

8. a: you / <u>agree</u> on this price
   b: no / my husband and I / already <u>tell</u> your
   salesman that we don't want to pay
   extra for an air conditioner that we don't need

9. a: you / <u>finish</u> reading the contract / yet
   b: yes, and / we / <u>find</u> several things that we
   need to discuss

___***C.**   **Beyond the book: With a partner, make questions and answers about your own life with words from the lists below and words of your own. Use the present perfect tense.**

EXAMPLE: **a:** Have you ever read a "how to" book?
   b: Well, I've often read "how to" books in my language, but I haven't read one in English yet.

ever	own a car
already	negotiate to buy something in this country
yet	read a "how to" book
before	fix a car
still	take a car for a test drive in this country
ever	read a consumer magazine
never	check a consumer magazine before buying something
often	

PART THREE / The Present Perfect and Simple Past Tenses: Review

● Describing Problems with Cars

Present Perfect	Simple Past
You can use the present perfect for an action happening now when you mention when it began (with *since*) or how long it has gone on (with *for*).	We can use the simple past in a clause with *since* that shows the beginning of the present perfect action.
He's worked here since last month. He's worked here for a month.	He's worked here since Ernie hired him.
	You can use the simple past tense with *for* to show the duration of an action that is finished.
	He worked at another car dealership for several years. (He doesn't work there now.)
You can use the present perfect tense for a finished action if the period of time in which it happened is not finished.	You can use the simple past tense for a finished action if the period of time in which it happened is finished.
They've sold 23 cars this month.	They sold 47 cars last month.
You can use the present perfect tense for an action at an unspecified time in the past with such words as *ever, yet, never, still,* and *already*.	You can use the simple past tense for an action at a specified time in the past with such expressions as *yesterday, at 2:00, last weekend, six years ago,* and *when I was a child*.

Although we usually use the present perfect tense with the words *recently* and *just*, it is possible to use the simple past tense with these words.

I've just bought a new car.
I just bought a new car.

A. Make sentences with the cue words. Use the present, present perfect, and simple past tenses. Follow the example.

EXAMPLE: 1. **a:** I'm really tired. I went to four used car lots yesterday, and I've gone to five more today.
  b: How come? Didn't you buy a car last week?
  a: Yes, but I still haven't sold the old one.

1. **a:** (I) tired
    (I) go to four used car lots yesterday / five more today
  b: (you) not buy a car last week
  a: (I) still not sell the old one

2. **a:** (my husband and I) angry
    (our new car) break down once last month / three more times this month
  b: (your mechanic) check it out before you bought it
  a: (he) not ever find all of its problems

3. **a:** (I) worried
    (I) have to call the department of motor vehicles twice last week / again this week
  b: (you) send them a check for your car registration last month
  a: (they) not send me my sticker yet

4. a: (I) upset

(my car insurance) go up last year / again this year, too

   b: (you) "shop around" to find the cheapest company

   a: (I) have several traffic tickets in the past year

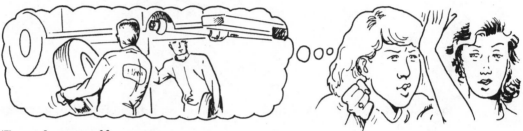

5. a: (I) mad at myself

(I) have a flat tire last month / two more this month

   b: (they) put four new tires on your car last year

   a: (I) not ever take the car back to the shop to have them rotate the tires

6. a: (I) upset

(I) get a speeding ticket a few weeks ago / two more just this week

   b: (you) pay attention to the speed limit signs

   a: (I) not fix my speedometer yet

7. a: (my cousin) in trouble

(he) try to bribe a police officer last month / again this month, too

   b: (you) explain to him that bribery is a serious crime in this country

   a: (he) never completely understand that law

B.   **Find and correct the mistakes in verb tenses in the following paragraphs.**

EXAMPLE: It's a good thing that my husband and I joined an automobile club last year.

It's a good thing that my husband and I have joined an automobile club last year. This car gave us a lot of trouble ever since we've bought it. Last March, for example, the battery has gone dead, so I've called the auto club, they've come, and they've started the car for me. In the past month, I have trouble with the carburetor several times. My mechanic already rebuilt the carburetor once, but this doesn't seem to help.

This time it seems to be more serious. About an hour ago, I've been on the highway when the car has begun to make strange noises. Of course, I've pulled over and called for help on a call box. I've waited for about thirty minutes, and then the auto club mechanic arrived. I never was so happy to see a mechanic in my whole life. I wasn't ever so wet or cold or miserable.

I gave this situation a lot of thought in the past hour, and I already made a decision. Of course, I didn't have a chance yet to tell my husband, but I decided that we need to sell this "lemon."

*C.   **Beyond the book: Think of something (or someone!) that has given you a lot of trouble in the past year or so. For example, you might choose your car, your motorcycle, your apartment, your health, your landlord, or your neighbor. Then either write a paragraph about your problem or tell a partner about it. Be sure to use the present perfect and simple past tenses correctly.**

EXAMPLE: I've had several problems with my landlord in the past year. Although I've asked him three times to fix my kitchen sink, he hasn't done anything yet. He came to look at it once a few months ago, but he hasn't been back since then.

PART FOUR / Prepositions of Place

● Telling Where Places Are

Following are some prepositions of place and some of their meanings:

Preposition	Meaning	Use
1. across (the street, the river, etc.) from	on the other side	The drugstore is across the street from the movie theater.
2. around the corner from	on a street that crosses the one where something else is	The fast food stand is around the corner from the used car lot.
3. between	at an intermediate place in relation to two other places or things	The movie theater is between the supermarket and the restaurant.
4. down the street from	a general phrase meaning "somewhere on the same street"	The hair salon is down the street from the supermarket.
5. kitty-corner from	on the opposite corner, diagonally	The library is kitty-corner from the video store.
6. next (door) to	beside	The video store is next door to the clinic.
7. in	inside a closed area (such as a room or building)	She works in the bakery on the corner.
8. around	from place to place	It's easy to get around by bus.

Other prepositions of place are *at* and *on*. *At* indicates a point or general area: at the corner, at the bank. *On* indicates "along" (on Edgeware Drive) or a specific point (on the corner of Main and 2nd).

A. **Look on the next page at the map of one section of Anita's and Richard's town. Then fill in the blanks with the correct prepositions from the box above.**

EXAMPLE: 1. The drugstore is around the corner from her house.

Anita doesn't really need a car because most of the places she goes to often are near her home.

The drugstore, for example, is _____ her house, and the post office is
                                       1.

_____ the drugstore. The supermarket where she shops is just
2.

_____ the post office. She lives only three blocks _____ the
3.   4.

bank, and the bank is _____ the best hardware store in town. Her son's high
                       5.

school is _____ the hardware store. She is taking a typing class at the adult
          6.

school _____ the high school. Whenever Anita has time, she tries to go to the
        7.

health club, _____ her adult school. Her daughter attends the elementary
             8.

school _____ Edgeware Drive, just _____ the health club.
        9.   10.

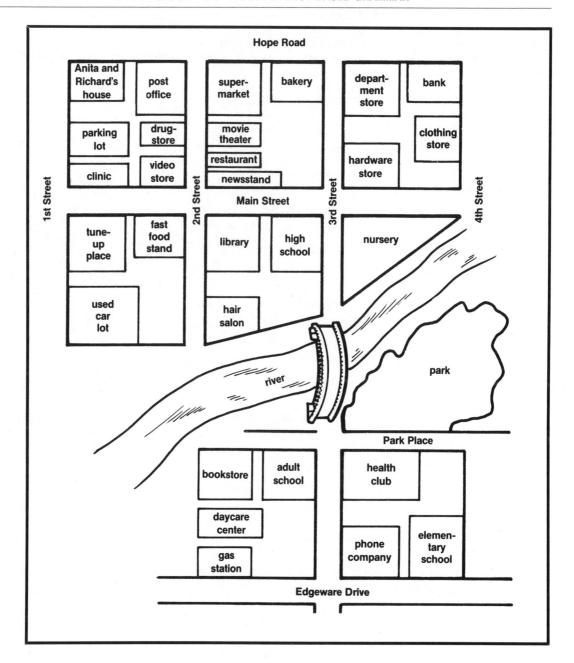

_____ **B.** With a partner, ask and answer questions about the map. Ask questions that your partner can answer by using the prepositions of place listed in the box on page 107.

EXAMPLE: a: Where's the hair salon in relation to the supermarket?
b: It's down the street from the supermarket.

_____ ***C.** Beyond the book: Draw a map of your neighborhood or the neighborhood around your school. Tell a partner where each place is. Use the prepositions of place from page 107.

EXAMPLE: My house is on Big Sky Drive, across the street from a park.

CHAPTER 7

Social Interaction

GRAMMAR:

The future in the past:
  was / were going to, would
The past perfect tense
Complex modals
The comparative and
  superlative of adjectives

COMPETENCIES:

Making excuses
Giving reasons
Discussing expectations of
  social situations
Understanding some social
  and dating customs
Making guesses about past
  actions
Giving advice about social
  situations
Comparing people

How much do you already know? Read the following conversation and choose the correct words. Circle your answers.

Elsa: Sometimes I get so confused! When I was in my country, I [knew/had known] the
         1.
         social "rules" of friendship and dating, but things are different here. I'm trying to be

         open to new ideas, but it's [more difficult/most difficult] than I thought it [was/
         2.   3.
         would be]. There are all sorts of problems. For example, when I first arrived here,

         I [never thought/had never thought] of calling a man before! Women in my
         4.
         country don't do that. And I [didn't ever drink/hadn't ever drunk] beer at a party
                                       5.
         because in my country it's a "man's drink."

Tomomi: I know what you mean. Two years ago, when I [found out/was going to find out]
                                                        6.
         that my husband and I [came/were going to come] to the United States, I quickly
                                7.
         enrolled in an English class. So when I [got/had gotten] here, I [already studied/
                                                  8.   9.
         had already studied] American culture. Even so, I felt uncomfortable the first time

         I went to a business dinner with my husband. Wives don't usually go to such parties

         in my country. I was nervous before the party! I [was/had been] afraid that I
                                                           10.
         [said/would say] something wrong!
         11.

Elsa: (*nods*) Yes. It is difficult. One custom that I didn't understand at first was "going

Dutch." It seemed like the [stranger/strangest] custom in the world for each
                              12.

person to pay for himself or herself when friends go out together—and often on a

date, too! (*Sighs.*) In fact, so many things seemed strange to me that I was very

unhappy. I [went back/was going to go back] to my country, but then I [started/
             13.   14.

had started] to make friends here, and life got [easier/more easy]. I decided to
                                                  15.

stay.

Tomomi: Uh-huh. Friends make a big difference. I think I [should have/could have] gotten
                                                            16.

into a lot of trouble without my American friend, Gail. She helped me figure out a

lot of the customs here. Also, I [shouldn't have/might not have] had the chance to
                                  17.

meet other Americans without her introductions.

Elsa: You're lucky. I was too shy at first to make friends outside of school. I guess I

[should have/may have] tried harder. I [shouldn't have/couldn't have] given up so
18.   19.

easily.

Tomomi: Well, I don't know about that. I think you just [should have/may have] been going
                                                           20.

through culture shock.

score: _____
                                                                                        20

PART ONE / The Future in the Past: *was / were going to, would*

● Making Excuses ● Giving Reasons ● Discussing Expectations of Social Situations

---

The Future in the Past: *was / were going to*

Subject	*be (not)*	*going to*	Verb
I	wasn't	going to	call him.
You	were	going to	help us.
She	was	going to	pay the bill.
They	weren't	going to	stay here.

Use the future in the past for an action that someone planned to do but never actually did.

> She was going to ask for a beer, but she didn't.

Use the simple past tense for: (1) the reason the action never happened or (2) what happened instead of the planned action.

> She was going to ask for beer, but then she <u>remembered</u> that women in that country didn't usually drink beer, so she <u>ordered</u> wine, instead.

A.

Make sentences with the cue words. Use the future in the past for each verb in the left-hand column. (This is the planned action that never happened.) Use the simple past tense for the verb in the right-hand column. (This is the reason that it didn't happen.)

EXAMPLE: 1. I was going to call you, but I forgot.

Action That Didn't Happen	**Reason**
1. I / call you	I / forget
2. she / pay for lunch	he / not let her
3. he / get tickets for a play	he / not have any money
4. we / make a reservation	they / say it wasn't necessary
5. he / invite her to a movie	he / be too shy
6. they / not go to the party	they / think it was rude to refuse
7. I / take wine to the host	I / not be sure if he drank alcohol
8. she / not invite him to a movie	her American friend / say it was okay to do so

_____ ***B.** **Beyond the book: What were some of your plans that didn't work out? Make as many sentences about them as possible. Use the future in the past (for the planned action that didn't happen) and the simple past tense (for the reason that it didn't happen or for what you did instead).**

EXAMPLE: I was going to invite him for coffee after class, but I was too shy.

The Future in the Past: _was/were going to, would_

You can also use the future in the past to express an action that someone thought was going to happen at some time after he or she thought it. The word _that_ is optional in such sentences.

I thought (that) life was going to be easy here.

Possible verbs besides _thought_ are:

believed	hoped
complained	imagined
doubted	knew
dreamed	never dreamed (= had no idea)
explained	realized
figured (= thought)	remembered
forgot	said/told
found out	suspected
guessed	was/were sure
had no idea (= didn't know at all)	

Another form of the future in the past is _would_ + the simple form.

I thought (that) life would be easy here.

_____ **C.** **Complete the sentences with the correct forms of the verbs in parentheses. Use the future in the past and the simple past tenses. Follow the example.**

EXAMPLE: **1. a:** What did you think he would say?
  b: Well, I thought that he was going to suggest a movie and dinner, but I didn't know we would go dancing too!

1. **a:** What _____ you _____ (think) he

_____ (say)?

  b: Well, I _____ (think) he _____

(suggest) a movie and dinner, but I _____ (not know) we

_____ (go) dancing, too!

2. a: What _____ you _____ (believe) your

life _____ (be) like here?

b: Well, I _____ (think) it _____ (be) a

little hard to meet people, but I _____ (never dream) it

_____ (be) so hard to make friends!

3. a: What _____ she _____ (hope) her

social life _____ (be) like?

b: Well, she _____ (hope) people _____

(drop by) to visit often, but she _____ (not know) they

_____ (usually call) first to make an appointment!

4. a: What _____ he _____ (think) everyone

_____ (talk) about?

b: Well, he _____ (figure) everyone _____

(discuss) politics, but he _____ (not suspect) the discussions

_____ (become) unpleasant arguments!

5. a: What _____ you _____ (think) that

you and your date _____ (talk) about?

b: Well, I _____ (figure) we _____

(just make) small talk, but I _____ (have no idea) he

_____ (ask) about religion!

6. a: What _____ Gail _____ (think) she

_____ (say) to refuse his invitation?

b: Well, she _____ (tell) me that she _____

(just say), "I'm sorry. I'm busy that evening." She _____

(never dream) he _____ (tell) her to choose any evening

when she wasn't busy!

7. a: What _____ he _____ (imagine) he

_____ (do) when the waitress brought the check?

b: Well, he _____ (figure) he _____ (pay) it.

He _____ (have no idea) that Gail _____

(offer) to pay half!

*D.   **Beyond the book: Have you experienced any of the following situations in the United States? What did you expect would happen? What actually happened? Were you surprised? Use the future in the past to tell or write about your expectations and the simple past tense to tell what really happened.**

a party with North Americans
a date
a snack after class with classmates
a business lunch/dinner
a visit with a neighbor

PART TWO / The Past Perfect Tense

● Understand Some Social and Dating Customs

The Past Perfect Tense

Subject	*had* (*not*)	Past Participle
I	had	called her before.
You	hadn't	met him.
They	had already	had several dates.

You can use the past perfect tense when you speak or write in the past tense and then "jump back" to an earlier action.

> I was surprised that he had asked that. (= First, he asked that. Then I was surprised.)

The adverbs below usually come between *had* and the past participle in affirmative statements.

> *recently   just   already   never*

I've never been there.

Still comes before *hadn't*.

> I still hadn't gone to the doctor for a checkup at that time.

Yet and *before* usually come at the end of a sentence.

> Had you done your exercises yet?
> Had you ever been there before?

Ever is usually used in questions and comes before the past participle.

With the present perfect tense (Chapter 6), all of these words (*recently, just, already, never, still, yet, before, ever*) mean "before now." With the past perfect tense, they mean "before then."

A. Use the cue words to make sentences about some common American attitudes (ideas) about social relations. Use the simple past tense for the verbs in the left-hand column and the past perfect for verbs in the right-hand column.

EXAMPLE: **1.** He introduced us because we hadn't met yet.

1. he / introduce us	because	we / not meet yet
2. I / be surprised when they dropped by	because	they / not call first
3. I / be glad to see them	although	I / not know they were coming
4. she / say that she couldn't go to dinner with him	because	she / already make plans
5. she / tell him that she couldn't go out with him	although	she / not really make other plans
6. she / think he was impolite	because	he / whistle at her on the street
7. she / not mind	although	he / not open the car door for her
8. he / get irritated with her	because	she / mention his weight
9. they / not be very close friends of ours	although	we / be to each other's homes for dinner
10. he / thank her	because	she / hold the door open for him
11. I / say "excuse me"	because	I / bump into him
12. he / be pleased	because	she / invite him to a movie
13. he / think that she didn't like him	because	she / say, "Sorry, I'm busy" to three of his invitations
14. she / call to ask him out	because	she / not be able to accept his invitations
15. Bill's girlfriend / not be jealous	although	Bill / meet his friend Ellen for coffee the day before

*B. Beyond the book: How many of the attitudes in Exercise A are common in your country? Which ones seem strange or different to you? For each that is different from an attitude in your country, change the sentence so that it reflects your culture.

EXAMPLES: **2.** I wasn't surprised when they dropped by although they hadn't called first.

12. He thought she wasn't very feminine because she had invited him to a movie.

_____ C. In the following story, Tomomi's American friend, Gail, is telling Tomomi about her difficulty with Greg. Greg wants to go out with Gail, but she doesn't want to go out with him. For each blank, choose the correct tense: simple past, future in the past, or past perfect.

EXAMPLE:
1. When Greg called me a few days ago,
2. I was really surprised
3. because I had just met him at work a few days before,
4. and I hadn't liked him very much.

When Greg _____ me a few days ago, I _____ really surprised because I
      1. call   **2.** be

_____ him at work a few days before, and I _____ him very much.
3. just meet   **4.** not like

Also, I _____ that he _____ me.
      5. not think   **6.** like

When he _____ me to go out on Saturday night, I _____ sort of uncomfortable
      7. ask   **8.** feel

and _____ to go. Unfortunately, I _____ with the situation very
      9. not want   **10.** not deal

well. I _____ him that I couldn't make it on Saturday because I _____ my
      11. tell   **12.** visit

parents that evening. Actually, this wasn't true, but I _____ an excuse not to go out with him.
                                                    13. need

Then he _____ about Sunday night. He _____ that he _____
      14. ask   **15.** say   **16.** get

tickets for the new play at the Sherwin Theater. So I _____ again and _____ him that
                                                    17. lie   **18.** tell

I _____ it. Then he _____ about my schedule two weeks from Saturday. I
  19. already see   **20.** ask

_____ to bite my fingernails from nervousness. I _____ him to ask a third
21. begin   **22.** not expect

time! Well, I _____ him for his kindness but _____ that I _____
          23. thank   **24.** explain   **25.** already make

plans for that evening. I _____ that I _____ out of town that weekend.
                      26. say   **27.** be

Well, you won't believe this, but then he _____, "How about a month from next Friday?"
                                          28. say

I _____ I _____! I _____ and _____ "okay." So now I have to
29. think **30.** scream   **31.** give up   **32.** say

go to a movie with him next month!

PART THREE / Complex Modals

● Making Guesses about Past Actions ● Giving Advice about Social Situations

---

Complex Modals: Possibility, Probability, Advice, Impossibility

You can express past possibility, probability, and advice with the same modals that you studied in Chapter 2: *may, might,* and *could* (for possibility), *must* (for probability), and *should* (for advice).

Subject	Modal	(*not*)	*have*	Past Participle
I	may		have	forgotten. (= Maybe I forgot.)
You	might	not	have	met him. (= Maybe you didn't meet him.)
He	could		have	known them. (= Maybe he knew them.)
We	must		have	left it there. (= Probably we left it there.)
Elsa	must	not	have	brought it. (= Probably Elsa didn't bring it.)
You	shouldn't		have	said that.

You can also use these modals in the past continuous.

Subject	Modal	(*not*)	*have*	*been*	Verb-*ing*
He	might		have	been	lying. (= Maybe he was lying.)
They	must	not	have	been	getting along. (= Probably they weren't getting along.)

<u>May not have</u> + past participle and <u>might not have</u> + past participle both mean "maybe not." However, <u>couldn't have</u> + past participle means "definitely not." (He couldn't have done it. = It is absolutely impossible that he did it.)

 A. **Change each of the following sentences to a sentence that means the same thing. Use complex modals of possibility and probability. (In some cases, there are several correct answers.)**

EXAMPLE: **1.** He might not have realized that you were trying to refuse him gently.

1. Maybe he didn't realize that you were trying to refuse him gently. = _____

---

2. He probably felt uncomfortable, too. = _____

_____

3. Maybe he was hoping that you'd change your mind. = _____

_____

4. It's absolutely impossible that he misunderstood. = _____

_____

5. He probably thought you were either very busy or very rude. = _____

_____

6. Maybe she lost your phone number. = _____

_____

7. Maybe she didn't want to hurt your feelings. = _____

_____

8. It's absolutely impossible that she was actually busy on three different evenings. =

_____

_____

9. She was probably making excuses. = _____

_____

10. She probably didn't realize what a great guy you are. = _____

_____

B. Use your knowledge of American culture to make sentences of past advice in the following situations. (There are several possible answers for each situation.)

EXAMPLES: **Situation 1:** She should have offered to pay half.
She shouldn't have let her friend pay the whole bill.

Situation 1: Tomomi went out to lunch with a friend. When the bill came, she let her friend pay.

_____

_____

Situation 2: Gail didn't want to go out with Greg, so she made up excuses and said that she was busy when she really wasn't.

_____

_____

Situation 3: Greg asked Gail out for several different evenings. Each time, she had a reason for not going. He thought, "Either she doesn't want to go out with me, or she does want to go but I've chosen evenings when she really can't."

_____

_____

Situation 4: A man received an invitation to a party at a friend's home. He wanted to bring his girlfriend with him, but he wasn't sure if that was proper.

_____

_____

Situation 5: A student from another country had lived in the United States for six months. He knew a few neighbors, classmates, and coworkers, but he didn't know them well. He just knew them well enough to make small talk. The student was lonely because his close friends were all back in his country.

_____

_____

Situation 6: A man was in a restaurant for lunch one day. He was with several people from his office. Suddenly he saw his girlfriend (whom he had known for three months) at a table with another man. He was very angry and went over to their table. She smiled and introduced the two men. She explained that the other man was an old friend whom she had known for years.

_____

_____

*C. Beyond the book: Imagine that the situations in Exercise B took place in your country. Use your knowledge of your own culture to make sentences of past advice for the same situations.

EXAMPLE: **Situation 1:** She should have simply thanked her friend and offered to take her to lunch another day.

D. Gail and Greg went out together, and, surprisingly, they both had a good time. They went to see a murder mystery. Unfortunately, they missed the beginning of the film. Then, near the end of the movie, the film broke, so they didn't see the end, either. Afterwards, they tried to figure out what had happened. What did they say? Read the following paragraph about the movie and then answer the questions. Use complex modals of possibility, probability, and advice in your answers. Make as many sentences as possible for each question.

EXAMPLE: 1. It could have been snowing, but it might have been raining.

¹It was a dark and stormy night. ²In a big house high on top of a hill, a man was lying on the floor. ³There was a butcher knife through his heart. ⁴His body was cold. ⁵A dog sat next to the man; the dog was whining. ⁶A window was broken, and the front door was open. ⁷There was a scent of perfume in the air. ⁸The maid was on the phone; she was hysterical.

1. **a:** Was it snowing? _____

_____

b: Was there a moon? _____

_____

2.   Why was the man lying on the floor? _____

_____

3. a: What room was he in? _____

_____

   b: What condition was he in? _____

_____

4. a: Why was his body cold? _____

_____

   b: How did he die? _____

_____

5.   Whose dog was it? _____

_____

6. a: How did the murderer get into the house? _____

_____

   b: How did the murderer leave? _____

_____

7.   Whose perfume was it? _____

_____

8. a: Why was the maid hysterical? _____

_____

   b: Who was she calling? _____

_____

*E.   **Beyond the book: Turn on your T.V. set to any comedy or drama, but turn down the sound so that you can't hear anything. Watch the show for fifteen minutes. Then try to guess what was happening. Make sentences about your guesses using complex modals of possibility, probability, and advice.**

EXAMPLE: The young woman was frowning, so she must have been angry. Her boyfriend might have forgotten their date. She should have waited a little longer for him.

PART FOUR / The Comparative and Superlative of Adjectives

● Comparing People

The Comparative and Superlative of Adjectives

You can use the comparative form (with *than*) for two things, people, or situations.

> Tomomi is taller than Gail.
> Her English is better now than it's ever been.

You can use the superlative form for three or more things or people.

> Elsa is the tallest of all.

One-syllable adjectives end in *-er* in the comparative and *-est* in the superlative.

> tall ⟶ taller than/the tallest
> wide ⟶ wider than/the widest

Adjectives with three or more syllables take *more...than* in the comparative and *the most...* in the superlative.

> unfortunate ⟶ more unfortunate than/the most unfortunate
> attractive ⟶ more attractive than/the most attractive

There are several rules for two-syllable adjectives.

1. Most two-syllable adjectives take *more than* and *the most*, especially those that end in *-ous, -ed, -est, -ing, -al,* or *-ful.*

   > formal ⟶ more formal/the most formal
   > worried ⟶ more worried/the most worried

2. Adjectives that end in *-y* change the *y* to *i* and take *-er* and *-est*:

   > happy ⟶ happier than/the happiest
   > foggy ⟶ foggier than/the foggiest

3. Some two-syllable adjectives can take either form. Examples of such adjectives are: *simple, angry, friendly, handsome, polite, quiet, stupid.*

   > simple { simpler than/the simplest
   > { more simple than/the most simple

There are also a few adjectives with irregular comparative and superlative forms:

> bad ⟶ worse than/the worst
> good ⟶ better than/the best
> far ⟶ farther than/the farthest
> little ⟶ less than/the least
> (= not much)

A. Compare the following people on "'The Date Finders," a T.V. game show. Use the comparative and superlative forms of the adjectives below.

EXAMPLE: Alex is shorter than Phil.
Dan is the shortest.

handsome	heavy	uncomfortable
generous	short	interesting
bald	wealthy	casual in appearance
polite	relaxed	

Phil

6'1"

wears jeans and a T-shirt

makes $21,000 a year

gives a lot of money to
homeless people

190 lbs.

gardener

never smokes near other
people

Alex

5'11"

wears slacks and a sport shirt

makes $15,000 a year

sometimes gives a little
money away

160 lbs.

movie actor

smokes anywhere he wants to

Dan

5'8"

wears a suit and tie

makes $30,000 a year

never gives any money to
homeless people

140 lbs.

librarian

asks permission before he
smokes

B. **For each blank below, choose either the comparative or superlative form of the adjective in parentheses.**

EXAMPLE: 1. I've just had the most interesting evening of my life!

I've just had _____ evening of my life! I'm _____ than
             1. interesting   **2.** happy

I've been for a long time. Greg is _____ person that I've ever met. At
                                 3. surprising

first, I thought he was _____ person in the world. Then I realized that
                       4. impolite

he's just _____ than most people. When he feels comfortable with you, he can tell
        5. quiet

_____ stories you've ever heard. I think he's a lot _____ than any
6. amazing   **7.** kind

other man I've gone out with. He's _____ person I know. And on top of
                           8. thoughtful

that, he's a _____ dancer than I am! We saw _____ movie
            9. good   **10.** bad

that I've seen in years, but I still had _____ time of my life. At the
                          11. enjoyable

restaurant, the waiter was _____ person you can imagine, and the service was
                    12. lazy

_____ I've ever experienced. The food was _____ stuff that I have
13. slow   **14.** terrible

ever eaten. But I still had _____ evening imaginable. I guess I'm in love!
                     15. wonderful

*C. **Beyond the book: Think of three people you know. Tell a partner a little about each of them, and then your partner will ask you questions about them. The questions and answers should include comparatives and superlatives.**

EXAMPLES: Which one is the most intelligent?
Is Alice nicer than Beth?

CHAPTER 8

Home and Family Life

GRAMMAR:
Infinitives (after verbs, for indirect speech, of purpose)
Gerunds (after prepositions, after certain verbs)
Infinitives or gerunds with similiar meanings
Infinitives or gerunds with different meanings
Go/take + gerund

COMPETENCIES:
Comparing the advantages of renting vs. owning a home
Buying a house
Moving
Fixing up a house
Finding child care
Getting information about senior citizen centers
Getting information about home care for the elderly
Getting information about activities through the YMCA and senior centers

How much do you already know? **Read the following paragraphs and choose the correct words. Circle your answers.**

Yoon Kwan Han and his family have been thinking of [look/looking] for a house to buy. They
                                                        1.
have been considering [to buy/buying] their own place ever since Yoon's brother moved in with
                        2.
them last year. There are now three adults and four children living in a small apartment, and the

rent keeps [to go/going] up every year.
              3.

Although they need more space and dislike [to argue/arguing] with a landlord who refuses
                                             4.
[to fix/fixing] things, they're afraid that they can't afford a house. They enjoy [to walk/walking]
5.   6.
around neighborhoods that they like, and they sometimes write down phone numbers of real estate

offices when they walk past "For Sale" signs in front of nice houses. But they're always shocked at

the prices. They remember [see/seeing] much bigger houses at lower prices back in their country,
                            7.
so sometimes they get discouraged.

Yoon's cousin, who is a real estate agent, has told them [not to/don't] hope for a "dream house."
                                                           8.
He tells them [to look/look] for a "fixer upper"—a house in bad condition. He says that they should
               9.
expect [to do/doing] a lot of work on their first house and *make* it nice.
        10.
Yoon's wife, Kyung Sook, is planning on [go/going] [to job hunt/job hunting] if they really
                                          11.   12.
do decide to buy a house because she knows it'll be difficult to pay the bills with just her husband's

paycheck. She worries about [leave/leaving] her children while she's at work, and she doesn't look
                             13.
forward to [try/trying] to find child care for them. But her sister has promised [to help/helping]
            14.   15.
her.

Kyung Sook is also worried about her aunt, who lives alone in another city. The woman likes

living alone, but she is elderly and not always well. Kyung Sook hopes [to find/finding] someone
                                                                        16.
to help her aunt with the [cook and clean/cooking and cleaning]. Also, she wants her aunt [to get/
                           17.   18.
getting] out of the apartment from time to time, go [to shop/shopping] or meet with other senior
                                                     19.
citizens. Kyung Sook has asked her husband [to help/help] her find a senior citizen center for her
                                            20.
aunt.

score: _____

20

PART ONE / Infinitives (after Verbs, for Indirect Speech, of Purpose)

● Comparing the Advantages of Renting vs. Owning a Home ● Buying a House

---

Infinitives after Verbs

Certain verbs usually take an infinitive (*to* + simple form) as an object. Some verbs that require infinitives are:

agree	intend
appear	know how
attempt	mean (= intend)
be able	neglect
care	offer
consent	plan
decide	pretend
fail	refuse
forget	seem
hope	

They hope <u>to buy</u> a house someday.

Certain other verbs take a noun (or pronoun) and then an infinitive. Some of these verbs are:

advise	permit
allow	persuade
cause	remind
convince	require
encourage	teach
force	tell
get (= persuade)	urge
invite	warn
order (= command)	

His cousin convinced <u>him to buy</u> a house while the interest rates were low.

Certain other verbs can take either (1) an infinitive or (2) a noun (or pronoun) and then an infinitive[1]. Some of these verbs are:

ask (= request)	promise
expect	want
need	would like

He wants <u>to find</u> a house soon.   or   He wants <u>his cousin to find</u> a house soon.

[1] The "short form" of a sentence with one of these verbs can end after the word *to*. **Example:**   Are you going to meet with the realtor today? Yes, we'd like to.

A. Complete the following paragraph with infinitives. Choose from the simple forms in the list below. (You may use a verb more than one time.)

EXAMPLE: **1.** Yoon's cousin, Jin, has been trying to persuade Yoon and Kyung Sook to buy their own house.

be	decide	move	save	spend
buy	keep	pay	sit	

Yoon's cousin, Jin, has been trying to persuade Yoon and Kyung Sook _____ their own house. Of course, they want _____ out of their small apartment, and they'd like

_____ free of the landlord, but they aren't sure that they'll be able _____

enough money for the down-payment and the monthly payments.

Jin, who is a realtor, has advised them _____ down and write out a list of all their

income (the money that they make) and all their expenses (the money that they need _____

each month). This list will allow them _____ how much money they can spend on a

house. Jin says they should plan _____ no more than 25 percent (%) of their income on

their house payments. Also, he has explained that they should expect _____ 10

percent (%) of the price of the house as a down-payment, so he is encouraging them _____

this money now.

Yoon and Kyung Sook are very nervous about all of this, but Jin is a very persuasive person.

He tells them _____ in mind the fact that home ownership will allow them

_____ a lot of money each year on income taxes.

Infinitives for Indirect Speech

You can use an infinitive to report a person's command (order).

"Make a list of your income and expenses," he said to them.
  = He told them <u>to make</u> a list of their income and expenses.

In the negative form, *not* comes before the infinitive.

"Don't expect too much," she said.
  = She said <u>not to expect</u> too much.

B. **What did Yoon's cousin tell him and his family to do? Make sentences; use indirect speech and infinitives.**

EXAMPLE: **1.** Yoon's cousin told them to take their time to shop for a house.

1. "Take your time to shop for a house."

2. "Consider the advantages of an older home."

3. "Don't expect to find a perfect house."

4. "Try not to spend more than 25 percent (%) of your income on house payments."

5. "Remember that the location is more important than the house itself."

6. "Look for the cheapest possible house in the best possible area."

7. "Try to imagine the house after you fix it up."

8. "Don't hire someone to paint the house when you can do it yourselves."

9. "Don't buy a house with serious problems with the heating, plumbing, or roofing."

10. "Call many different banks to find the lowest interest rates for your loan."

11. "Have an inspector check any house that you might seriously want to buy."

Infinitives of Purpose

Infinitives often show purpose; that is, the infinitive may answer the question "Why?"

> He called the real estate office <u>to ask</u> about a house.
> (Why did he call? Because he wanted to ask about a house.)

C. Match the activities in the left-hand column with the purpose for them in the right-hand column. Then make new sentences with infinitives.

EXAMPLE: **1.** They decided to buy a house to save money on income taxes.

1. They decided to buy a house.

2. He drove them around the city.

3. The realtor put all of their figures into a computer.

4. She called her friends.

5. They called an inspector.

6. They made an appointment with the loan officer of the bank.

7. The realtor went to see the sellers of the house.

8. They stayed home all day Saturday.

a. He showed them the areas that they could afford.

b. She told them that she and Yoon had found a house.

c. They wanted to save money on income taxes.

d. They discussed the different possible types of home loans.

e. He needed to find out how much they could spend on a house.

f. He checked the condition of the house.

g. They filled out the loan application at their kitchen table.

h. He put an offer on their house.

*D. Beyond the book: If you're renting an apartment or house, tell or write the answers to these questions. Use infinitives in your answers.

1. Why did you decide to rent?

2. Do you hope to buy a house someday?

3. What does your landlord (or landlady) permit you to do? What doesn't he/she permit you to do?

4. What do you expect the landlord/landlady to fix?

5. Is there anything that you can't get your landlord/landlady to fix?

6. Where would you like to live?

7. Has anyone ever given you advice about buying a house? If so, what did this person tell you to do or not to do?

If you own your own house, tell or write the answers to these questions.

1. Why did you decide to buy a house?

2. Do you plan to stay in this house or move to another?

3. What would you like to do to improve your home?

4. Do you do some repairs on your house yourself, or do you ask someone else to fix things?

5. If you have a garden, how much time do you need to spend on yardwork?

6. When you were looking for a house to buy, did anyone give you advice? If so, what did this person tell you to do or not to do?

PART TWO / Gerunds (after Prepositions, after Certain Verbs)

● Moving ● Fixing Up a House

Gerunds after Prepositions

A gerund (verb-*ing*) is a verb form that takes the place of a noun. A gerund is sometimes the object of a preposition.

> We were nervous <u>about moving</u>.
> She was tired <u>of packing</u>.

You can also use a gerund after these expressions:

> be used to (= be in the habit of)
> be accustomed to (= be used to)
> get used to (= become used to)
> look forward to (= anticipate with pleasure)
> feel up to (= feel well enough, be in the mood for)
> object to (= be against, feel dislike for)

They <u>look forward to having</u> a backyard.

A gerund sometimes follows the preposition *by* to show the way that something is done. That is, *by* + gerund may answer the question "How?"

> He found the least expensive moving company <u>by calling</u> every mover in the phone book. (How did he find an inexpensive moving company? He called every one in the phone book.)

A. **Fill in the blanks with gerund forms. Choose from the verbs in the list below. (You may use a verb more than once.)**

EXAMPLES: **1.** After signing the last loan papers,
2. the Hans began to get excited about moving into their new home.

call	find	have	hire	pack	sign	take
fill	go	help	move	rent	spend	

After _____ the last loan papers, the Hans began to get excited about
        1.

_____ into their new home. They had thought about _____ movers, but
2.   3.

Yoon objected to _____ so much money, so they finally decided on _____
                 4.   5.

a truck and _____ themselves. They had succeeded in _____ dozens of
            6.   7.

boxes at local supermarkets and liquor stores, and the whole family worked hard

at _____ for a week before they moved. Kyung Sook took care of _____
    8.   9.

the phone company, the water company, and the gas and electric company because

she was anxious about _____ these utilities from the first day in the new
                           10.

house. Yoon was responsible for _____ to the post office and _____ out
                                 11.   12.

a change of address card.

    Several of the Hans' friends appeared early in the morning on moving day and

insisted on _____ them move. The Hans were very grateful for their help.
            13.

The move took only five hours instead of _____ all day.
                                          14.

Gerunds after Certain Verbs

A verb must be in the gerund form after one of these verbs or expressions:

appreciate	consider	finish	imagine	spend time
avoid	deny	get through	involve	suggest
can't help	enjoy	(= finish)	mind	
(= can't avoid)	feel like	have trouble	postpone	

She <u>considered taking</u> a "how to" class.
They <u>didn't mind spending</u> time on their house.

B. Answer the questions about the Hans' first month in their new house. Use the cue words and gerunds. Each conversation is in the past tense. Follow the example.

EXAMPLE: **1. a:** How did you learn so much about home improvement?
      b. By reading these "how to"[1] books. I didn't feel like taking "how to" classes.

1. a: How did you learn so much about home improvement?
  b. read these "how to" books
    (I) not feel like / take "how to" classes

2. a: How were you able to afford to buy a house?
  b. buy a "fixer-upper"
    (we) can't keep / rent anymore

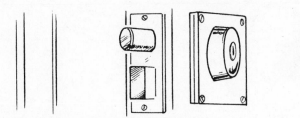

3. a: How did they make the house safe?
  b. put dead-bolt locks on the doors and special locks on the windows
    (they) not want to postpone / do this

---

[1]This isn't a complete sentence, but in conversation it's the natural answer to such a question. The complete sentence is: I learned about it by reading these "how to" books.

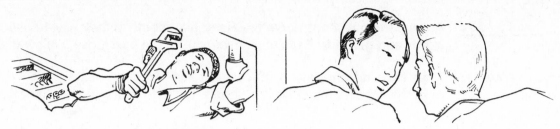

4. a: How were you able to find a good plumber?
   b. ask friends for recommendations
      (we) appreciate / get their suggestions

5. a: How did we spend so much money in one week?
   b. buy a million small things for the house
      (we) can't avoid / buy these necessary things

6. a: How did you improve the yard in such a short time?
   b. hire some teenagers from the neighborhood one weekend
      (they) not mind / make a little extra money

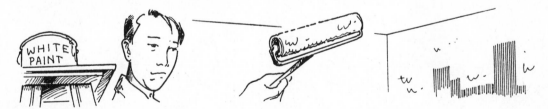

7. a: How did Yoon make this room seem larger?
   b. paint it white
      (he) finish / paint it just yesterday

8. a: How were they able to afford so many repairs?
   b. do most of the work themselves
      (it) involve / spend a lot of time and energy, though

_____ ***C.** **Beyond the book: Finish these sentences with information about the apartment or house where you live. Use gerunds.**

EXAMPLE: **1.** I found my apartment by looking through the classified ads in the newspaper.

1. I found my apartment (house) by _____.

2. I (We) sometimes have trouble _____.

3. I'd like to postpone _____.

4. There's no way to avoid _____.

5. I try to keep my house safe by _____.

6. I don't usually mind _____.

7. My landlord/landlady/manager/neighbor insists on _____.

8. I never feel like _____.

9. My landlord/landlady/doesn't seem to care about _____.

10. I make my apartment (house) feel like "home" by _____.

PART THREE / Infinitives or Gerunds with Similiar Meanings

● Finding Child Care ● Getting Information about Senior Citizen Centers

---

Infinitives or Gerunds with Similiar Meanings (I)

A verb after one of these verbs may be either an infinitive or a gerund. There is little or no difference in meaning.

begin	hate	prefer
can't stand	like	start
continue	love	try

A. **Choose the correct form of each verb: an infinitive or a gerund. (In a few cases, both answers would be correct.)**

Soon after _moving_ into their new neighborhood, Kyung Sook started _____ for a
1. move   2. look

day-care center for her two youngest children. She didn't have to worry about _____
                                                                                                                   3. find

child care for the older kids because they would be able _____ in the after-school
                                                                                                       4. stay

program at their public school. This allowed her _____ them up at 5:30, after work.
                                                                                      5. pick

But she expected _____ some trouble _____ a good center for the younger
                                       6. have   7. find

two, and she didn't look forward to _____ such an important decision.
                                                                 8. make

She began _____ for a child-care center by _____ the YWCA, a local church, and
                       9. look   10. call

the pediatric department of a hospital because she wanted _____ for a list of nearby centers.
                                                                                               11. ask

Also, she hoped _____ some advice on _____ the best possible one.
                               12. get   13. choose

She appreciated _____ a pamphlet from the local hospital because it gave some
                                14. receive

specific suggestions. It advised her _____ four or five centers based on their location,
                                                           15. select

cost, hours, and size. Then, it said, she should visit each one and not consider _____ her
                                                                                                                    16. send

children to a center that didn't permit parents _____. At each center, she ought to see
                                                                            17. visit

if the children liked _____ there and if there were interesting activities, clean rooms, and
                        18. be

friendly teachers. Before _____ a decision, the pamphlet said, she should sit down and ask
                          19. make

the director about meals, naps, toys, and extra clothes for the children as well as first-aid training

and licensing of the staff members. Finally, the pamphlet told her _____ her children
                                                                    20. not enroll

at any day-care center that didn't allow them _____ a special "security toy."
                                              21. bring

Infinitives or Gerunds with Similiar Meanings (II)

A gerund can be the subject of a sentence. You can rephrase such a sentence to mean the same thing by using the subject *it* and an infinitive.

Finding a senior citizen center is a good idea for an elderly person.
(= It's a good idea for an elderly person to find a senior citizen's center.)

B. Make new sentences that have the same meaning as the following sentences. Use gerunds as subjects.

EXAMPLE: **1.** Living alone isn't much fun.

1. It isn't much fun to live alone.
2. It's not enjoyable to eat by yourself.
3. It's difficult to find someone who will help with housework.
4. It's depressing to be alone.
5. It's expensive to go out for a little fun these days.

1. Yes, that's true. _____

_____

2. You're right. _____

_____

3. I know. _____

_____

4. I agree. _____

_____

5. That's certainly true. _____

_____

Now make new sentences that have the same meaning as the following sentences. Use *it* and an infinitive.

EXAMPLE: **1.** It might be a good idea to join the local senior center.

6. Joining the local senior center might be a good idea.

7. Meeting other people at the center would be very nice.

8. Having a hot meal every day is possible at senior centers.

9. Taking classes at the center could be interesting.

10. Enjoying ourselves isn't all that expensive at a senior center

6. I suppose you're right. _____ _____

7. Yes, that's true. _____ _____

8. I've heard that, too. _____ _____

9. Maybe you're right. _____ _____

10. That's what Mrs. Allan said. _____ _____

_____ ***C.**   **Beyond the book: Make sentences about your opinions on family activities. Use the verbs below and infinitives or gerunds. (You can work in small groups.)**

EXAMPLE: I can't stand doing the dishes every night.

can't stand	hate	like	love	prefer

_____ ***D.**   **Beyond the book: Tell or write about some difficulties you have had with children, parents, or the elderly. Use infinitives and gerunds.**

EXAMPLES: Finding a child-care center isn't easy.

It's hard to have a full-time job and a family, too.

PART FOUR

Infinitives or Gerunds with Different Meanings; *go* / *take* + Gerund

● Getting Information about Home Care for the Elderly ● Getting Information about activities through the YMCA and Senior Centers

---

Infinitives or Gerunds with Different Meanings

A verb after one of these verbs may be in either the infinitive or gerund form. However, the meaning is not the same.

forget   regret   remember   stop

She remembered <u>to call</u> her aunt.
  (= First, she remembered. Then she called.)

She remembered <u>calling</u> her aunt.
  (= She remembered that she had called.)

She stopped <u>to call</u> her aunt.
  (= She stopped doing something else because she wanted to call her aunt.)

She stopped <u>calling</u> her aunt.
  (= She used to call her aunt, but she doesn't now.)

_____ **A.** **Choose the correct form of each verb: an infinitive or a gerund.**

EXAMPLE: **1. a:** Do you remember asking me for information about someone to help Mrs. Allan at home?

a: Do you remember _____ me for information about someone to help
                  1. ask

Mrs. Allan at home?

b: Of course. I remember _____ you that she needs some help with cooking,
                    2. tell

cleaning, and bathing because of her broken arm. Have you found someone?

a: Well, yes . . . and no. It seems that there are lots of people who do this work, but I

regret _____ that medical insurance—including Medicare—doesn't pay for it.
        3. say

b: Oh, that's right. I had forgotten. I remember _____ one time that insurance
                    4. hear

covers these services only if the person also needs a nurse.

a: (*Sighs.*) Yes. Isn't that terrible? But listen! A few days ago I heard about a program

that might be perfect for her. I simply forgot _____ you when we talked
                    5. tell

yesterday. I really regret _____ to mention it. I'm sorry that . . .
                6. not think

b: Please stop _____! Just tell me about the program!
         7. apologize

a: Well, it seems that some hospitals have something called a senior companion

program. Anyway, I have a pamphlet that has more information. Maybe we can

stop _____ it to Mrs. Allan right now.
      8. give

b: Oh, not now. We'll be late for the movie. But let's remember _____
                        9. stop

at her house on the way home.

a: Okay. If this program works out, we can stop _____ about her.
                    10. worry

---

go/*take* + gerund

The gerund form usually follows the verbs *go* and *take*[1] (someone):

bowl	fish	hunt	mountain-climb	shop	swim
camp	hike	ice-skate	roller-skate	skate	water-ski
dance	house-hunt	jog	sail	ski	window-shop

They went shopping[2].   He often takes her dancing.

[1] If the action is happening right now, use the present continuous tense. Don't use *go* + gerund. **Examples:** They're shopping. He's dancing with her.

[2] The infinitive form of one of these verbs after *go* shows purpose. However, this usage is not very common. **Example:** They went to shop for a shirt. = They went shopping because they wanted to shop for a shirt.

B. Use these words to make sentences about activities at the YMCA and at a local senior citizens' center. Use *go* or *take* with the gerund form of verbs from the list in the box above. Follow the example.

EXAMPLE: **a:** Where did Sammy go?
b: He went camping. The YMCA takes a group of kids camping every summer.

1. **a:** Sammy
   b: the YMCA / a group of kids / every summer

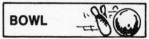
CAMP

2. **a:** Billy
   b: the YMCA / a bunch of kids / once a month

SKATE

3. **a:** Mrs. Elliot
   b: the seniors' center / a group of people / every Friday

BOWL

4. **a:** Armen and Rafik
   b: the YMCA / groups of children / from time to time

HIKE

5. **a:** Sarah and Al
   b: the senior citizens' center / them / once a week

SHOP

6. **a:** the kids
   b: the YMCA / them / as often as possible

SWIM

*C. Beyond the book: What do you remember doing as a child? Make sentences about your own life. (You can work in small groups.)

EXAMPLE: I remember going fishing with my grandfather.

Work and Money

GRAMMAR:
The present conditional:
   factual and imaginative;
   wish
The past conditional:
   factual and imaginative;
   wish
Indirect statements
Embedded questions
Indirect questions

COMPETENCIES:
Comparing jobs and
   choosing a type of work
Discussing strategies for job
   interviews
Getting a business loan
Discussing safety in the
   workplace

How much do you already know? **Read the following conversation, and choose the correct words. Circle your answers.**

Nikos: (*looking over cards on the "Job Openings" board*) Gosh, I wish I [can/could] find a
1.

job.

Tran: I thought you said that your uncle [will/would] give you a job in his restaurant. If I
2.

[have/had] an offer like that, I wouldn't be looking for a job! I wish I [was/were]
3.   4.

in your shoes!

Nikos: I know, I know. But I've been working in restaurants for almost ten years. It's time for a change. I'm not sure what [I want/do I want] to do with my life, but I'm
5.
pretty sure that I don't want a career in the restaurant business.

Luis: A lot of people are changing careers these days. There are even "career counselors" to help you decide. If I [knew/had known] about career counselors when I was
6.
back in my country, maybe I [would choose/would have chosen] a different line of
7.
work.

Nikos: Yeah, but counseling is expensive. I asked a few counselors how much [it would
8.
cost/would it cost], and I found out that I just can't afford it. I wish I [saved/had
9.
saved] more money when I had a job.

Tran: (sighs) Me too. I [will open/would open] a small business if I could just save
10.
enough money.

Luis: Do you know what [you should/should you] do? You ought to go to a bank and ask
11.
about a business loan. Ask a loan officer what [he thinks/does he think] about your
12.
chances of getting a loan.

Tran: Maybe I will. It can't hurt to ask.

Nikos: (picks up some pamphlets on a table) Hey, look at these: "How to Get and Keep a Job," "Choosing the Right Career for You," "Running a Small Business," and "Job Interviews." (sighs) If I [had/had had] this pamphlet before that interview last
13.
week, I [wouldn't be/wouldn't have been] so unprepared.
14.

Luis: I asked you [if you wanted/did you want] to practice before you went to the
15.
interview, but you said you [don't need/didn't need] to practice.
16.

Nikos: (shakes his head sadly) I wish I [listened/had listened] to you. That was my fourth
17.
unsuccessful interview in a week.

Tran: If I [were/was] you, I [will/would] take that job with your uncle, at least for a
18.   19.
few months. You need some time to figure out what kind of job [you're going/are
20.
you going] to look for—and how to get it.

score: _____

20

PART ONE / The Present Conditional: Factual and Imaginative; *wish*

● Comparing Jobs and Choosing a Type of Work

The Present Conditional: Factual

A factual conditional sentence in the present tense has two clauses: one with the cause or condition and the other with a result, possibility, probability, advice or a command.

> If you take some courses, you will get a job.
> (cause)   (result)

> If it's 11:00, Nikos must be arriving for his appointment.
> (condition)   (probability)

The order of the two clauses may be reversed:

> You will get a job if you take some courses.
> (result)   (cause)

The verb in the *if* clause is in the simple present or present continuous tense. In the other clause, there is either a simple modal, the present tense, or a command.

A. **Here are some things that career counselors often tell people. Make conditional sentences with the modal *should*. Match the phrases from the left-hand column with appropriate advice from the right-hand column.**

EXAMPLE: 1. If he isn't happy with his job, he should decide what kind of work he enjoys instead.

1. not be happy with his or her job
2. like the work but not the boss
3. decide to change careers
4. not know much about certain jobs
5. not have the skills for the job he or she wants
6. want a "dream job"

a. make a list of his or her abilities, skills, and interests
b. go back to school part time
c. decide what kind of work he or she enjoys instead
d. not wait around for it; go and get it
e. ask people who are doing them
f. check into changing to a different department in the company

The Present Conditional: Imaginative

An imaginative conditional sentence expresses the opposite of the true situation.

I don't have a good job offer, so ——→ If I had a good job offer, I
I need to keep my present job.   wouldn't need to keep my
(true situation)   present job.   (conditional)

In the conditional sentence above, the cause (condition) is in the first clause and the result is in the second.

I need to fill out this   ——→ I wouldn't need to fill out this
questionnaire because I want   questionnaire if I didn't want
to figure out my "dream job."   to figure out my "dream job."
(true situation)   (conditional)

In the conditional sentence above, the result is in the first clause and the cause (condition) is in the second.

In the imaginative present conditional, the simple past or past continuous tense is in the *if* clause.[1] (The meaning is present.) *Would, (could, might)* + the simple form of the verb are in the other clause. Notice that an affirmative clause in the true situation becomes negative in the conditional, and a negative clause in the true situation becomes affirmative in the conditional.

[1] If the verb is *be*, all persons take *were* in the *if* clause. **Example:** If I were you, I would (I'd) figure out exactly what kind of job makes me happiest.

B. **Make new sentences that change the following true situations to the conditional. Keep the clauses in the same order as in the sentences below. Follow the example.**

EXAMPLES: 1. If I knew what to do with my life, I wouldn't be here at this job counseling workshop.
2. I wouldn't be working at a job that I hate if I weren't afraid to quit.

1. I don't know what to do with my life, so I'm here at this job counseling workshop.

2. I'm working at a job that I hate because I'm afraid to quit.

3. I'm a woman, so it's difficult to get work in the construction business.

4. I work because I have to earn money for my family.

5. I'm not happy because I don't own my own business.

6. Job security is really important to me, so I'm staying at that company.

7. My English isn't good, so I'm nervous about job interviews.

8. I won't quit and try something new because I have to support my family.

9. I can't find a computer-training course that meets on Saturdays, so I'm not taking one this semester.

---

wish

When you want something now (in the present) that you believe is impossible or is the opposite of the true situation, you can use *wish* and the past tense.

I have to work late every night. (true situation)	→ I wish I <u>didn't have</u> to work late every night.
My job isn't near my home. (true situation)	→ I wish my job <u>were</u> near my home.

 C. **Use the cue words to make sentences about the wishes of people who are unhappy with their job situations.**

EXAMPLES: **1.** Jean wishes she didn't work late every night.
She wishes she liked her boss.

1. works late every night
doesn't like her boss
has to be nice to impolite customers
needs to be on her feet for eight hours
is bored with her job

JEAN

2. has to carry a heavy pack
doesn't like to work in cold weather
dogs bite him
is tired all the time
catches colds on rainy days

TOM

3. doesn't get to travel on the job
can't be outside on a nice day
has to be very careful about counting money
needs to be patient when customers get angry
doesn't meet interesting people

ELLIE

4. ?????
?????
?????
?????
?????

YOU OR SOMEONE YOU KNOW

*D. **Beyond the book: Check (√) your answers on the questionnaire below. Then work with a partner and make questions and answers using the imaginative conditional.**

EXAMPLES: a: If you could work anywhere, what kind of place would you choose?
b: If I could work anywhere, I'd choose the sporting goods department of a big store.

QUESTIONNAIRE: A DREAM JOB

What's Important to You?

The first step in finding a job that you enjoy is to decide what's important to you. This questionnaire will help you discover the kind of work that would make you happiest.

Place:

☐ outdoors   ☐ in a store   ☐ at home   ☐ on a plane, ship, or train

☐ in an office   ☐ in a factory   ☐ in a studio   ☐ other

Salary:

☐ high salary / no vacation pay or health benefits
☐ low salary / good health benefits
☐ medium salary / some health benefits

Type of Work:

☐ working with people
☐ working with tools, machines, or equipment
☐ working with information
☐ doing artistic work (painting, music, writing, etc.)
☐ other

Most Important to Me:

☐ salary   ☐ hours
☐ interest in the work   ☐ nice co-workers
☐ good location, beautiful office   ☐ a job with a good future
☐ benefits   ☐ other

PART TWO / The Past Conditional: Factual and Imaginative; *wish*

● Discussing Strategies for Job Interviews

The Past Conditional: Factual

A factual conditional sentence in the past tense has two clauses: one with the cause or condition and the other with the result. Both clauses are in the past tense.

If he thought about his job interview, he began to get nervous.
     (cause)   (result)

In these past conditional sentences, *if* often means *when*.

A. Tom was looking for a job last year. He was very careful and well organized, and he was offered a job after just a few interviews. How did he manage to do so well? Match phrases from the right-hand column to those in the left-hand column. Make factual conditional sentences in the past.

EXAMPLE: 1. If he knew he was going to have an interview the next day, he went to sleep early and got up early.

1. know he was going to have an interview the next day

2. think he would need names and addresses for the application form

3. not be sure where the office was

4. have an interview for an office job

5. have an interview for a job as a driver

6. need to be at an interview at 10:00 o'clock

a. go a day before to find it

b. try to get there a few minutes early

c. go to sleep early and get up early

d. wear a sport shirt and a jacket

e. bring the information with him on index cards

f. wear a business suit and a tie

The Past Conditional: Imaginative

As in the present conditional, an imaginative past conditional sentence expresses the opposite of the true situation. An affirmative clause in the true situation becomes negative in the conditional, and a negative clause in the true situation becomes affirmative in the conditional.

He was late to his interview, so the secretary canceled his appointment.   (true situation) ⟶ If he hadn't been late to his interview, the secretary wouldn't have canceled his appointment. (conditional)

or:

⟶ The secretary wouldn't have canceled his appointment if he hadn't been late to his interview.

The cause (in the *if* clause) is in the past perfect or past perfect continuous tense. The result (in the other clause) is expressed with *would(n't)* (*may, might, could, should*) *have* + the past participle.

B.

Make sentences that express the opposite of these people's experiences in job interviews. Use the imaginative past conditional (with *would have* or a complex modal of possibility) for the result clause and the past perfect continuous tense for the *if* clause. Follow the example.

EXAMPLES: 1. Bob wouldn't have gotten the job if he hadn't shown interest in the company. If he hadn't had a firm handshake and made eye contact, he might not have gotten the job.

1. Bob got the job.
   He showed interest in the company.
   He had a firm handshake and made eye contact.
   He didn't chew gum or smoke in the interview.
   His past employers gave him good recommendations.

2. They didn't hire Alice.
   She didn't seem to enjoy that sort of work.
   She wore noisy, jangling earrings and bracelets.
   She was chewing gum during the interview.
   She didn't have a firm handshake or make eye contact.

3. Karen's interview went well.
   She was on time.
   She filled in the application form neatly and completely.
   She had two years of experience doing similiar work.
   She emphasized that she enjoyed her work.

4. Alan's interview didn't go well.
   He said a lot of negative things about his past employers.
   He didn't answer all of the questions on the application form.
   He was mainly interested in an easy job.
   He wasn't listening as the interviewer explained the job.

> ### *wish*
>
> When you want something that happened in the past to be different from the true situation, you can use *wish* and the past perfect or past perfect continuous tense.
>
> | | | |
> |---|---|---|
> | I didn't say the right things in the job interview. (true situation) | ⟶ | I wish I <u>had said</u> the right things. |
> | I was late for the interview. (true situation) | ⟶ | I wish I <u>hadn't been</u> late for the interview. |

C.   **Make sentences with *wish* about the following true situations. Follow the example.**

EXAMPLE: **1.** I wish I hadn't gotten to the interview so early.

1. I got to the interview forty-five minutes early.

2. The waiting made me nervous.

3. I didn't bring names and addresses to the interview.

4. I asked the receptionist for a telephone book.

5. I made mistakes on the application form and crossed them out.

6. I didn't say more than "yes" or "no" in the interview.

7. I didn't tell the interviewer about my part-time job in high school.

8. My hands were shaking all through the interview.

9. I told all my friends that I'd get this job.

10. I didn't get the job.

*D.   **Beyond the book: Tell or write about job interviews that you've had. What happened? Do you wish that something had happened differently? Use the imaginative past conditional and *wish* + the past perfect tense.**

EXAMPLES: If my friend hadn't told me about the job opening, I wouldn't have known about the interview.

I wish I had prepared better for the interview.

PART THREE / Indirect Statements

● Getting a Business Loan

Indirect Statements

Indirect speech or reported speech tells what someone said. If the direct quotation is a statement, there is sometimes a change of tense in the indirect quotation.

> "I need to borrow some money," he said.
> = He said (that[1]) he <u>needed</u> to borrow some money.

Some general rules for verb usage in indirect speech are as follows:

Direct Speech		**Indirect Speech**
simple present	⟶	simple past
present continuous	⟶	past continuous
simple past	⟶	past perfect
past continuous	⟶	past perfect continuous
present perfect (continuous)	⟶	past perfect (continuous)
past perfect (continuous)	⟶	(no change)
may	⟶	*might / could* (possibility)
can	⟶	*could*
will	⟶	*would*
must (= *have to*)	⟶	*had to*
must (= probably)	⟶	(no change)
should	⟶	(no change)

The tense doesn't always have to change. For example, if the direct quotation expresses a general truth, the tense does not change.

> "Water freezes at 32°," said the teacher.
> = The teacher said that water <u>freezes</u> at 32°.

[1] The word *that* is optional.

A. **Make sentences about getting a loan. Change the direct quotations in the pictures to indirect speech. Follow the example.**

EXAMPLE: **1. a:** I talked with Tran the other day.
  b: Oh really? What did he say?
  a: He told me he had been thinking of applying for a business loan. He said he wanted to open a magazine stand.

  1. Tran

I've been thinking of applying for a business loan. I want to open a magazine stand.

2. my brother

It's a good idea to start by going to your own bank. You can explain your reason for wanting the money to the loan officer there.

3. the loan officer at my bank

You'll need to fill out a loan application form. It's important to answer every question completely and honestly.

4. my loan officer again

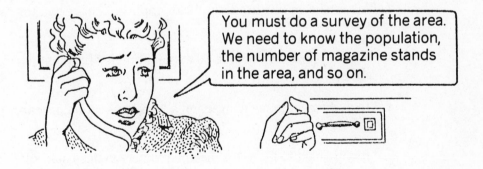

You must do a survey of the area. We need to know the population, the number of magazine stands in the area, and so on.

5. my friend John

I can help you with your loan application if you need it. You may have some trouble with it.

6. Tran again

I'm having some trouble with the loan application. I have to estimate my expenses and income taxes before the bank will accept my application.

7. my neighbors

The bank turned down our loan application last year. We found out why, corrected the problem, and tried again.

B. Here are some suggestions and information that a financial advisor on the radio recently gave his listeners when they asked about loan applications. Change each direct quotation to indirect speech.

EXAMPLE: **1.** He said the banker would probably check the information on a loan application with employers, other banks, and credit card companies.

1. "The bank will probably check the information on a loan application with employers, other banks, and credit card companies."

2. "Loan officers like to see that loan applicants have had the same job for more than five years."

3. "It's a good idea to include an explanation for frequent job changes or time without a job."

4. "Including company bonuses on a loan application probably won't make a difference."

5. "It can't hurt to list extra income if a person has listed such income on tax returns in the past two years."

6. "A long-term customer may get a better deal at his or her own bank."

*C. Beyond the book: Work in a group of three people. Talk about experiences you or someone you know has had with loan applications or with banks in general. One person will make a statement, another will pretend he or she didn't hear, and the third will repeat the statement with indirect speech.

EXAMPLE: **a:** I stood in line at the bank for thirty-five minutes yesterday.
b: What did he say?
c: He said that he had stood in line at the bank for thirty-five minutes yesterday.

PART FOUR / Embedded Questions; Indirect Questions

● Discussing Safety in the Workplace

Embedded Questions

An embedded question is "inside" another question or statement. Embedded questions have statement word order (subject/verb). They do not have the auxiliary verb *do*.

                 Question: When can he start?
Embedded Questions: Do you know <u>when he can start</u>?
                          I'm not sure <u>when he can start</u>.

                 Question: What time does the store open?
Embedded Questions: Can you tell me <u>what time the store opens</u>?
                          I don't know <u>what time the store opens</u>.

For questions that will have an answer of "yes" or "no" use the word *if* in the embedded question.

                 Question: Did he get to work on time?
Embedded Questions: Do you know <u>if he got to work on time</u>?
                          I have no idea <u>if he got to work on time</u>.

 A. **Make sentences that are useful in polite business telephone calls. Use the cue words and follow the example. Use embedded questions.**

EXAMPLE: **1.a:** Could you tell me if they have filled the position yet?
         b: I'm sorry. I don't know. I'll transfer you to the personnel office. Someone there can tell you if they've filled it.

   1. personnel office / someone there

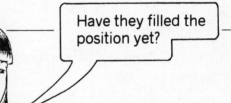

Have they filled the position yet?

   2. payroll office / Ms. Lopez

How should I fill out my W-4 form?

3. Mr. Albert / he

Who should I talk to about changing shifts?

4. your union representative / she

Do they deduct union dues from our paychecks?

5. his office / his secretary

Has Mr. Evans returned from lunch yet?

6. shipping and receiving / they

When did you ship our order?

7. the manager / he

Is it too late for me to change an order?

Indirect Questions

When you report a question that someone has asked, use the rules for an embedded question (see page 159). Usually the verb tense changes in the indirect quotation in the same way as the tense changes in indirect statements (see page 156).

"When will she return to the office?" he asked.
= He asked <u>when she would return</u> to the office.

"How many people has he interviewed?" I asked
= I asked <u>how many people he had interviewed</u>.

"Did they receive the order?" she asked.
= She asked <u>if they had received</u> the order.

B. **Make sentences describing the following conversations about safety rules in the workplace. Change each direct quotation to an indirect one and use embedded questions. Follow the example.**

EXAMPLE: 1. The supervisor told the new employee (that) she would need to tie her hair back and remove all jewelry. The employee asked him why that was important. He said hair and jewelry could get caught in the machine.

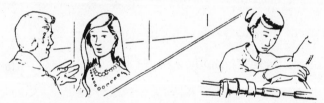

1. Supervisor: You'll need to tie your hair back and remove all jewelry.
New Employee: Why is that important?
Supervisor: Hair and jewelry can get caught in the machine.

2. Foreman: Where are your safety goggles?
Luisa: I think I left them in my locker.
Foreman: If you don't wear them, I won't let you operate this machine.

3. Supervisor: What's wrong?
Mark: I feel dizzy from breathing the fumes from this paint remover.
Supervisor: Why didn't you open a window? Paint remover can be dangerous in a room without fresh air.

4. Juan: Where can I go to report an unsafe condition?
Kien: You'll need to fill out a form and give it to the shop steward.
Juan: Does the boss get angry about these reports?
Kien: No. He wants to hear about any problem.

C. What did the following people ask? Change the direct quotations to indirect ones.

EXAMPLE: **1.** The foreman asked Bill if he knew how to operate a forklift.

1. "Do you know how to operate a forklift?" the foreman asked Bill.

2. "Where can I find a first-aid kit?" he asked.

3. "Why do I have to wear earplugs?" she asked.

4. "Is it safe to work in this area?" I asked.

5. "Does everyone need to wear a mask?" he asked.

6. "What day will the safety inspector be here?" she asked.

7. "Do you think there's enough light in the work area?" the safety inspector asked us.

8. "How did you hurt your back?" the doctor asked Juan.

9. "Why didn't you bend your knees in lifting that heavy box?" his friend asked him.

10. "Did you tell your supervisor about your accident?" I asked her.

11. "How often has it happened?" the inspector asked.

12. "Why is it so important to report injuries to the employer?" they asked.

*D. Beyond the book: In groups of three, ask questions about work and safety conditions in the places where you have worked. One person will pretend not to hear each question and the third person will repeat the question as an indirect question.

EXAMPLE: **a** (to **b**): Is there something dangerous about your work?
b (to **c**): What did she say?
c (to **b**): She asked you if there was something dangerous about your work.

CHAPTER
10

Education

GRAMMAR:
The passive voice:
  simple present and past
    tenses
  continuous and perfect
    tenses
  it + passive
  future tense and modals
Present and past participles
  as adjectives

COMPETENCIES:
Helping your children
  succeed
Identifying learning
  disabilities
Identifying gifted children
Understanding opportunities
  for continuing education

How much do you already know? **Read the following speech and choose the correct words. Circle your answers.**

"Ladies and gentlemen, you have [been calling/been called] here this evening to find out how
1.

your children can be [encourage/encouraged] to succeed in their studies—not only this school
2.

year, but in the future, too.

"Your children are [being/been] taught by some of the finest teachers in this state, but is this
3.

enough? No! It [often thinks/is often thought] that a child's education [acquires/is acquired] only
4.   5.

in school, but this isn't true. Children have their first experiences of life in the home. It is in the

home that they can learn to be [excited/exciting] [for/about] going to school. It is from their
6.   7.

parents that they can learn to be [interested/interesting] [in/by] reading, math, music, science,
8.   9.

art, and all of the other subjects that they will experience in school. Children [influence by/are
10.

influenced by] their home life.

"Of course, each child has individual needs. Some children need extra help with their studies;

they have special problems called learning disabilities. Classes [are providing/are provided] at
11.

this school to help these students. Other children are very intelligent in one or more subjects;

special help [needs/is needed] in such cases, also. These gifted children are often easily [bored/
12.   13.

boring] if they [aren't giving/aren't given] extra, more difficult work. This school offers a
14.

program for gifted children.

"But what might be [doing/done] at home, by parents, to help children do well in school?
15.

Well, later this evening, each of you will [give/be given] a pamphlet with a list of suggestions. But
16.

right now let me recommend making your home a good atmosphere for learning. In other words,

show your child that books can be [excited/exciting] and that libraries and museums are
17.

[fascinated/fascinating] places. Don't let your child be [frightened/frightening] of school. Set an
18.   19.

example for your child to follow. Take a class at your local adult school, YMCA, or college each

semester. Let it be [understand/understood] by all of your children that education is a lifelong
20.

process!"

PART ONE   The Passive Voice:
Simple Present and Simple Past Tenses

● Helping Your Children Succeed

The Passive Voice: Simple Present and Simple Past Tenses

In sentences in the active voice, the emphasis is on the subject (the person or thing that performs the action).

The teacher teaches study skills every semester. (active voice: *teacher* = subject; *study skills* = object) ⟶ Study skills are taught every semester. (passive voice: *study skills* = subject)

When you want to emphasize the object instead of the subject, you use the passive voice. In the passive voice, use the verb *be* and the past participle of the main verb. The verb *be* is in the same tense as the verb in the corresponding sentence in the active voice.

Teachers encourage parents to join the P.T.A.   (active voice) ⟶ Parents are encouraged to join the P.T.A.   (passive voice)

The teacher taught the students to read.   (active voice) ⟶ The students were taught to read.   (passive voice)

The schools give each student books to use.   (active voice) ⟶ Each student is given books to use.   (passive voice)

A. **Make sentences about Lisa and Eric Cox (students who are doing well in school) and John Bell (who isn't doing well). Use the cue words to explain how these students' parents influence their attitudes toward education. Use the passive voice in the present tense. Follow the example.**

EXAMPLE: **1.** Lisa and Eric are encouraged to turn off the T.V.
John isn't encouraged to turn off the T.V.

1. encourage to turn off the T.V.   not encourage to turn off the T.V.

2. give praise for good grades   not praise for doing well

3. not punish for a bad grade   punish for bad grades

4. teach how to use memory tricks   not teach how to use memory tricks

5. take to museums and libraries   not take to museums or libraries

6. tell not to let a difficult problem   allow to use any excuse to quit
be an excuse to quit

7. show how to break a big project   not help with organization of homework
into smaller parts

8. teach to use a dictionary and an atlas   not teach to use a dictionary or an atlas

9. encourage to ask questions   not encourage to ask questions

B. Make sentences about the same students when they are older. Use the passive voice in the simple past tense and use the cue words from Exercise A.

EXAMPLE: 1. Lisa and Eric were encouraged to turn off the T.V. John wasn't encouraged to turn off the T.V.

I dropped out of school and I can't find a job.

Using *by* + Subject

The passive voice is most often used in the following situations:

1. The subject (in the active voice) is not important to the meaning of the sentence.

   People appreciated the lecture. ———► The lecture was appreciated.

2. The subject is unknown (for example, *somebody*).

   Someone invited them to   ———► They were invited to a meeting.
   a meeting.

3. You want to avoid mentioning the subject.

   I stole my brother's book.   ———► My brother's book was stolen.

However, sometimes the subject (from the active voice) is included after the word *by*. Add *by* + subject in these situations:

1. the subject (in the active voice) is a proper name too important to leave out.

   The P.T.A. sent a newsletter   ———► A newsletter was sent to
   to everyone.   everyone <u>by the P.T.A.</u>

2. The subject gives new information.

   Two parents and a teacher   ———► The newsletter was written <u>by</u>
   who volunteered to produce   <u>two parents and a teacher who</u>
   it each month wrote the   <u>volunteered to produce it each</u>
   newsletter.   <u>month.</u>

_____ **C.** **Change each sentence in this P.T.A. newsletter from the active voice to the passive voice. Add *by* + subject only when necessary.**

EXAMPLE: A speech was given by Dr. Rowena Stone at the P.T.A. meeting on Tuesday.

Dr. Rowena Stone

Dr. Rowena Stone gave a speech at the P.T.A. meeting on Tuesday. She suggested several ways to help children succeed. She told the audience of about seventy-five people about "harmful" and "helpful" home situations.

People teach successful students to think for themselves and do their own homework. A wise parent limits a child's time in front of the T.V. He or she chooses good programs carefully. A lazy parent uses the T.V. as a "babysitter." He or she doesn't take care in choosing programs. Also, parents' reading habits influence children.

Dr. Stone's speech encouraged everyone. They asked a lot of questions afterwards. They formed discussion groups during the coffee hour.

_____ ***D.** **Beyond the book: Tell or write about how your children are helped educationally (if you are a parent) or how you were helped when you were a child (if you aren't a parent). Use the passive voice.**

EXAMPLES: My children aren't allowed to watch T.V. until they finish their homework.
When I was a child, I was encouraged to get my own library card.

PART TWO   The Passive Voice: Continuous and Perfect Tenses; *it* + Passive

● Identifying Learning Disabilities

The Passive Voice: Continuous and Perfect Tenses

The passive voice can also appear in the present continuous or past continuous tenses.

The school is offering special ⟶ Special classes are being offered
classes for students with by the school for students with
learning disabilities. learning disabilities.
(active voice) (passive voice)

They weren't offering such a ⟶ Such a class wasn't being offered
class when my grandmother when my grandmother
needed one.   (active voice) needed one.   (passive voice)

The passive voice can also appear in the present perfect or past perfect tenses. (However, it does not appear in the present perfect continuous or the past perfect continuous.)

They have tested many ⟶ Many students have been tested
students for learning for learning disorders.
disorders.   (active voice) (passive voice)

They had tested him for a ⟶ He had been tested for a
learning disability called learning disability called
dyslexia.   (active voice) dyslexia.   (passive voice)

 A.   **Change the following sentences from the active to the passive voice. Add** *by* **+ subject when necessary.**

EXAMPLE: **1.** Jimmy is now being given extra help for his learning disability.

1. They are now giving Jimmy extra help for his learning disability.

2. We had contacted our family doctor.

3. He had checked Jimmy's hearing and eyesight.

4. Federal law is requiring schools to test for learning disabilities.

5. People are making great efforts to discover children with learning disabilities.

6. Teachers are teaching Jimmy to tape-record his classes and type his homework.

Does Your Child Have a
LEARNING DISABILITY?

Warning Signs:

- doesn't listen well
- doesn't remember
- reads poorly
- writes poorly
- exchanges letters in words
- has trouble naming common things
- is behind age group in speech development
- is difficult to discipline

It + **Passive**

It plus the passive voice is sometimes used to avoid mentioning the subject from the active voice. With this construction, a clause with *that* sometimes follows one of these verbs: *believe, feel, find, hope, know, report, rumor, say,* or *think.*

People sometimes say that children with dyslexia are "stupid," but this isn't true. (active voice)	It is sometimes said that children with dyslexia are "stupid," but this isn't true. (passive voice)

_____ **B.**   **Make sentences with the verbs and clauses below. Use *it* + the passive voice.**

EXAMPLE: **1.** It is believed that one-tenth of all children in the United States have a learning disorder.

1. (believe) one-tenth of all children in the United States have a learning disorder

2. (believe) the most common learning disorder is dyslexia

3. (report) Albert Einstein and Thoman Edison had dyslexia

4. (know) dyslexia is not the result of low intelligence

5. (think) it's best for dyslexics to study in regular classrooms, if possible

6. (hope) a way of preventing dyslexia can be found

_____ ***C.**   **Beyond the book: Do you know anyone who has been found to have a learning disability? If so, tell about this person's experiences. If not, ask questions about another person's experiences. Use the passive voice.**

EXAMPLES: **a:** My little sister has been found to have a learning disability.
b: What has been done to help her?
a: She has been given a special class.

PART THREE / The Passive Voice: Future Tense and Modals

● Identifying Gifted Children

The Passive Voice: Future Tense and Modals

The passive voice can appear in the future tenses and with modals (*can, could, may, might, should, must*).

The school will (is going to) give tests to discover gifted children. (active voice)	⟶ Tests will (are going to) be given to discover gifted children. (passive voice)
People can't test a child for giftedness until he or she is three or four years old. (active voice)	⟶ A child can't be tested for giftedness until he or she is three or four years old. (passive voice)

A. **Make sentences about gifted children with the modals and phrases below. Use the passive voice.**

EXAMPLE: **1.** The Apgar test can be given at birth to measure a baby's development.

1. (can) the Apgar test / give at birth to measure a baby's development

2. (can) the Stanford-Binet Intelligence Test / give after four years of age

3. (may) children's behavior / observe to see if they have special abilities

4. (might) a sense of humor / develop at an early age

5. (may) ideas or objects / put together in creative ways by gifted children

B. How should gifted children be helped? Change the following suggestions from the active voice to the passive voice.

EXAMPLE: 1. Extra help and encouragement must be given to gifted children.

1. People must give extra help and encouragement to gifted children.

2. Someone should provide games, books, and musical instruments for gifted children.

3. Parents should take gifted children to the museum and library.

4. People must encourage a gifted child to have hobbies.

5. Parents must allow a gifted child to be a child—not a "small adult."

6. People should accept a gifted child as he or she is.

7. People should praise a gifted child for trying something new.

8. Parents must give love freely—not as a reward for good grades in school.

*C. Beyond the book: What do you think is important in children's education? What should be done to help any child? What can be done to help gifted children? Discuss or write about this topic. You can work in small groups.

EXAMPLES: I think children must be taught to respect life.
Gifted children should be allowed to have a lot of different experiences.

PART FOUR / Present and Past Participles as Adjectives

● Understanding Opportunities for Continuing Education

Present and Past Participles as Adjectives

Participles of certain verbs are often used as adjectives. Present participles
are used for the *cause* of an emotion; past participles are used for the result.
Prepositions sometimes follow the past participle. Some of these verbs and the
correct prepositions to use with them are:

Verb	Present Participle	Past Participle	(Preposition)
to amuse	amusing	amused	at/by/with
to annoy	annoying	annoyed	at/by/with
to bore	boring	bored	by/with
to confuse	confusing	confused	at/by
to disappoint	disappointing	disappointed	in/with
to disgust	disgusting	disgusted	at/by/with
to embarrass	embarrassing	embarrassed	about/by
to excite	exciting	excited	about
to exhaust	exhausting	exhausted	from
to fascinate	fascinating	fascinated	by
to frighten	frightening	frightened	by (specific)/of (general)
to interest	interesting	interested	in
to irritate	irritating	irritated	by/with
to puzzle	puzzling	puzzled	at/by
to shock	shocking	shocked	at/by
to surprise	surprising	surprised	at/by
to terrify	terrifying	terrified	by (specific)/of (general)
to tire	tiring	tired	from (physical exercise)/of

He thinks math is <u>interesting</u>.   (Math is the cause of the interest.)

He's <u>interested in</u> math.   (His interest is the result.)

Local adult schools and community colleges offer an <u>exciting</u> variety of free and
inexpensive classes.

We're <u>excited about</u> the possibility of continuing our education.

A. **Fill in the blanks with present or past participles of the verbs.**

EXAMPLE: **1.** Have you always been fascinated by psychology, astronomy, or history?

Have you ever wished that you could change careers, understand world politics, or learn a

musical instrument? Have you always been _____ by psychology, astronomy, or
1. fascinate

history? Have you sometimes been _____ to find that you can't help your child with
2. embarrass

a _____ math problem? Have you ever thought, "I'd like to go back to school, but I'm
    3. puzzle

just too old"?

    Well, don't be _____! It's never too late! You're never too old to continue your
       4. frighten

education. In cities and towns across North America, adults of all ages are discovering _____
                                                                5. surprise

possibilities in free and inexpensive classes for adults at local museums, YMCAs, community

colleges, parks and recreation departments, and adult schools. Several _____ classes
                                                  6. fascinate

are even offered on public television on subjects such as cooking, car repair, gardening,

photography, and the renovation or repair of old homes.

    You might be _____ by the variety of classes that are offered. Are you
            7. surprise

_____ in astronomy? Try the local museum or planetarium. Are world politics
8. interest

_____ to you? Take a class in current affairs at your local adult school. Is your dog's
9. confuse

behavior _____? Try a dog training class through the department of parks and
          10. irritate

recreation. Is your family _____ by the meals you serve? Take a cooking class at a
           11. bore

nearby community college.

    Best of all, perhaps, is the opportunity to meet people who share your interests. Adults from

many countries find that it's _____ to learn a new subject, practice English, and make
            12. excite

new friends at the same time.

B. **Make sentences about the biology class in the picture. Use the present and past participles of the verbs below. Use prepositions if necessary.**

EXAMPLES: 1. Carlos is excited about the lesson. He thinks biology is exciting. He isn't bored at all.

bore	disgust	excite	confuse
tire	fascinate	annoy	amuse

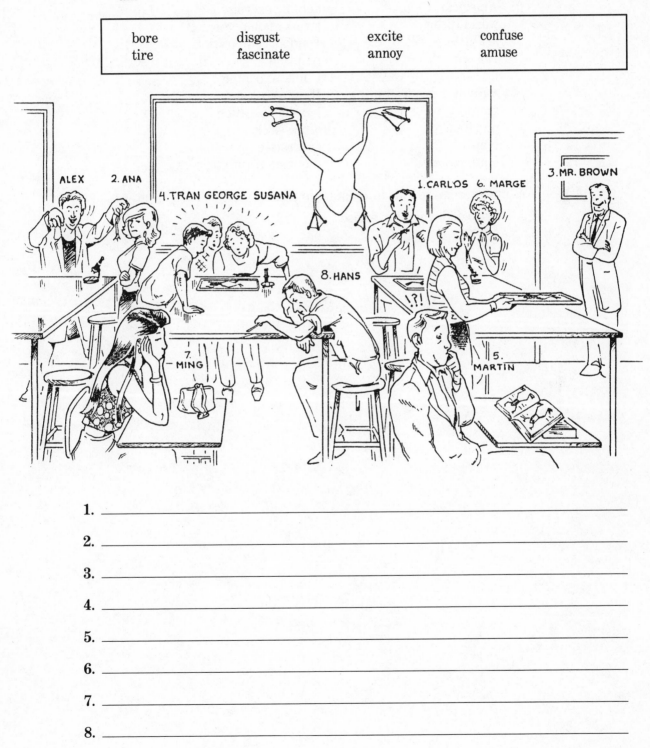

1. _____

2. _____

3. _____

4. _____

5. _____

6. _____

7. _____

8. _____

_____ *C.   **Beyond the book: Tell or write about your opinions of the following adult education subjects. Use present and past participles. You can work in small groups.**

photography	clothing design
American history	aerobic exercise
world history	stress management
art history	English composition
biology	painting
ice skating	Chinese cooking
computer programming	Italian cooking
guitar	parent education
nutrition	office skills
typing	real estate
math review	the restaurant business

EXAMPLES: Aerobic exercise sounds interesting to me.

I get exhausted when I exercise.

APPENDIX A

Common Irregular Verbs

be am-is-are, was-were, been
beat, beat, beaten
become, became, become
begin, began, begun
bend, bent, bent
bet, bet, bet
bleed, bled, bled
blow, blew, blown
break, broke, broken
bring, brought, brought
build, built, built
burst, burst, burst
buy, bought, bought
catch, caught, caught
choose, chose, chosen
come, came, come
cost, cost, cost
creep, crept, crept,
cut, cut, cut
dig, dug, dug
dive, dove *or* dived, dived
do, did, done
draw, drew, drawn
drink, drank, drunk
drive, drove, driven
eat, ate, eaten
fall, fell, fallen
feed, fed, fed
feel, felt, felt
fight, fought, fought
find, found, found
fit, fit, fit
flee, fled, fled
fly, flew, flown
forget, forgot, forgotten
freeze, froze, frozen

get, got, got *or* gotten
give, gave, given
go, went, gone
grind, ground, ground
grow, grew, grown
hang, hung, hung
have, had, had
hear, heard, heard
hide, hid, hidden
hit, hit, hit
hold, held, held
hurt, hurt, hurt
keep, kept, kept
know, knew, known
lay, laid, laid
lead, led, led
leave, left, left
lend, lent, lent
let, let, let
lie, lay, lain
lose, lost, lost
make, made, made
mean, meant, meant
meet, met, met
pay, paid, paid
put, put, put
read, read, read
ride, rode, ridden
ring, rang, rung
rise, rose, risen
run, ran, run
say, said, said
see, saw, seen
sell, sold, sold
send, sent, sent
set, set, set

sew, sewed, sewn
shake, shook, shaken
shine, shone, shone
shoot, shot, shot
show, showed, shown
shrink, shrank, shrunk
shut, shut, shut
sing, sang, sung
sink, sank, sunk
sit, sat, sat
sleep, slept, slept
speak, spoke, spoken
spend, spent, spent
split, split, split
spread, spread, spread
stand, stood, stood
steal, stole, stolen
stick, stuck, stuck
strike, struck, struck
swear, swore, sworn
sweep, swept, swept
swim, swam, swum
take, took, taken
teach, taught, taught
tear, tore, torn
tell, told, told
think, thought, thought
throw, threw, thrown
understand, understood, understood
wake, woke *or* waked, waked
wear, wore, worn
win, won, won
wind, wound, wound
write, wrote, written

APPENDIX B

Irregular Verb Groups

Sometimes it helps to learn irregular verbs in groups. It is easier to remember patterns than individual verbs. Some of the verbs in these groups are listed below.

Verbs with the same form for the simple form, past tense, and past participle:

bet	cost	hit	let	quit	shut	spread
burst	cut	hurt	put	set	split	

---

find—found—found
grind—ground—ground
wind—wound—wound

---

creep—crept—crept
sleep—slept—slept
sweep—swept—swept

---

lend—lent—lent
send—sent—sent
spend—spent—spent

---

slink—slunk—slunk
stick—stuck—stuck

---

bleed—bled—bled
feed—fed—fed
flee—fled—fled
lead—led—led
read—read—read

.. ..

lay—laid—laid
pay—paid—paid
say—said—said

.. ..

sell—sold—sold
tell—told—told

---

bring—brought—brought
buy—bought—bought
fight—fought—fought
think—thought—thought

catch—caught—caught
teach—taught—taught

---

drive—drove—driven
ride—rode—ridden
rise—rose—risen
write—wrote—written

---

blow—blew—blown
grow—grew—grown
know—knew—know
throw—threw—thrown

---

swear—swore—sworn
tear—tore—torn
wear—wore—worn

---

begin—began—begun
drink—drank—drunk
ring—rang—rung
shrink—shrank—shrunk
sing—sang—sung
sink—sank—sunk

---

freeze—froze—frozen
speak—spoke—spoken
steal—stole—stolen

---

shake—shook—shaken
take—took—taken